Wool-Gathering or Analysis

"In the small canon of literary works concerned with psychoanalysis, *Wool-Gathering* is a milestone because, unlike all previous efforts, it is funny and not earnest. This book manages to make the agonizing question of when to end the treatment hilarious without slagging the whole process off."

Oliver James

"Gunn has done something that few people have ever achieved: he has written an exceptionally perceptive account of the last few weeks of his analysis in a way that is both *gripping and entertaining*. His narrative approach, encompassing the hilarious aspects of his daily life in Paris as well as the more associative and probing work of analysis, makes for a page-turner that at the same time explores the psychoanalytic process in provocative ways."

Professor Bruce Fink, translator of Jacques Lacan's *Écrits*, Duquesne University, USA

"I cannot recall enjoying a new book as much as this for a long time. It is beautifully written, immensely engaging, very funny, very informative and, by the end, moving."

Professor Stephen Frosh, Birkbeck College, London

Wool-Gathering or How I Ended Analysis is a personal and humorous account of the last month of a psychoanalysis, principally Lacanian in orientation, taking place in a frenetic and strikebound Paris. A diary account, interspersed with a commentary on the analysis, *Wool-Gathering* is not only a highly entertaining memoir, but also a more meditated account of a process, opening up a world normally kept private in a new and engaging way.

Dan Gunn is Professor of Comparative Literature at The American University of Paris, and works as a writer, teacher, researcher, reviewer and editor.

Wool-Gathering or How I Ended Analysis

Dan Gunn

First published 2002 by Brunner-Routledge
27 Church Road, Hove, East Sussex BN3 2FA

Simultaneously published in the USA and Canada
by Taylor & Francis Inc.
29 West 35th Street, New York, NY 10001

Brunner-Routledge is an imprint of the Taylor & Francis Group

© 2002 Dan Gunn

Cover design by Jim Wilkie
Cover art: "His Hour" by R.B. Kitaj, 1975, charcoal and pastel
Typeset in Times by Mayhew Typesetting, Rhayader, Powys
Printed and bound in Great Britain by TJ International Ltd, Padstow, Cornwall

All rights reserved. No part of this book may be reprinted or
reproduced or utilized in any form or by any electronic, mechanical,
or other means, now known or hereafter invented, including
photocopying and recording, or in any information storage or
retrieval system, without permission in writing from the publishers.

British Library Cataloguing in Publication Data
A catalogue record for this book is available from the British Library

Library of Congress Cataloging-in-Publication Data
Gunn, Daniel.
    Wool-gathering or how I ended analysis / Dan Gunn.
        p. cm.
    Includes bibliographical references and index.
    ISBN 1-58391-278-9 – ISBN 1-58391-279-7 (pbk.)
    1. Gunn, Daniel. 2. Analysands–France–Biography.
3. Psychoanalysis–Case studies. I. Title.

RC464.G86 A3 2002
616.89'17–dc21   2002025856

ISBN 1-58391-278-9 (hbk)
ISBN 1-58391-279-7 (pbk)

To Toni

"Turn on the machine," says Lister.

Mr McGuire does so, and the bobbins go spinning.

"When I was a boy, fourteen," says Lister, "I decided to leave England. There was a bit of trouble over me having to do with Eleanor under the grand piano, she being my aunt and only nine. Dating from that traumatic experience, Eleanor conceived an inverted avuncular fixation, which is to say that she followed me up when she turned fourteen and —"

"It isn't right," says Mr McGuire, turning off the machine.

"It isn't true, but that's not to say it isn't right," Lister says.

Muriel Spark, *Not to Disturb*

We are all going to end some day or night: the problem being that, unless we are religious believers, we have no idea what this means. Is it ignorance in the face of this one crucial certainty that makes us concentrate so hard upon the endings which precede it, endings which we're convinced, by contrast, we should control, or at least rehearse thoroughly, or at very least understand?

"What a pity it had to end that way."

"Thank God it's over."

"Should never have started in the first place."

"Allows a new beginning."

"Finally let go."

"Finito!"

"Kaput."

They come in all shapes and sizes: of childhood, virginity, bachelorhood; of living at home, marriage, employment; of friendship, love, enmity; and of life as well of course – other people's lives. One tries to squeeze significance out of one's endings, like the last blobs from a tired tube of toothpaste (the old-fashioned kind that you could fold and torture). Unless it's the other way round, and one is actually trying to squeeze significance *into* them, yes, with as much difficulty as when trying to get the paste back into the tube (the old-fashioned kind again, it's not so hard with the modern plastic ones).

There's a certain sort of relationship that has an ending present from the outset, and that's the one established with a professional carer, whether doctor, surgeon, dentist, chiropodist, osteopath, or any other sort of therapist. For when turning to such carers, one does so hoping soon to be out of their hands, finding oneself more alive than before, ready to begin all sorts of new adventures.

And within this set of carers there's a certain type whose practice takes that ever-present ending and makes a meal of it. Not only because they're not permitted the laying on of hands, and so cause frustration from the outset (since in that interdiction there's lurking some sort of pre-inscribed ending). But also because if an ending ever does occur, then it will have been brought about by words, words spoken, among others, about what it means to end.

I had one month left to go in my analysis. But what did that mean?

I had one month left to go. But would I get out of it alive, let alone more alive than before? Would I ever get to an end, let alone THE END?

Tuesday 21 November 1995

If I'm going to start a journal, then let me at least try and get the simple things clear. Ten years I've lived in a flat in the African quarter of Paris known as the "Goutte d'Or", in the 18th arrondissement. Ever since I moved in, it's had water dripping through the ceiling from the Togolese family upstairs. Every so often I've tried to stop this flow, but never with enough determination. So that up until 7 weeks ago half my flat was a slum, the other half clean, organised, perfectly liveable-in.

Until the start of October, that was, when I bring in a builder to do up the slum side, presuming in some quite irrational way that this'll oblige my neighbours to fix their leaking shower.

Partitions are pulled down, pipes torn up. With no heating or water, I move out for what's supposed to be three weeks. The builder removes the plaster beneath the upstairs shower and passes his hand straight through the 14-inch-square oak beam that's been supporting the whole building for over 100 years.

Consequence: a rapid succession of meetings with insurance men, lawyers, engineers, architects, neighbours, a court case. And the likelihood that until the end of the year at least, for the remainder of my analysis therefore, I'll be living, in a literal and local way now as well as more metaphorically or broadly, <u>away from home</u>.

Consequence: my contemplating tonight of the imminent end of this 6-year-long psychoanalytic process isn't going on in even moderate tranquillity. I sit freezing in the building site my flat has become, after being ejected from . . . X's (?) flat today, where I've been taking refuge these past 7 weeks. No time today to make arrangements for other accommodation, with the rushing to work, forgetting notes, back home to fetch them, then out, forth, back, on, like a dervish carrying a dumb-bell in one hand.

So sudden that departure from X's today, after our 7 weeks' cohabitation: 15 minutes and everything turned around, I knew I'd have to leave. Packed belongings hastily into plastic bags, and, suddenly unwelcome, I was out of there. We'd never been ready to live together, and a generous offer on her part turned into a burden when the quick repairs to my flat became a protracted legal battle. She watched me leave, saying nothing. From the day after tomorrow I'll be able to stay at . . . Y's studio in the 20th arrondissement, since she's with her boyfriend up the road.

"X" will hardly do for the woman I'm passionate about (even if in my own thwarted way). She of the lightning temper and the thick black Basilicata hair. Of the frighteningly strong dancer's abductors and the occasional blind panic when she fears she's lost something (a panic so strong she'd rather throw it away than risk losing it later). Of the unplaceable accent and the mocking laugh. To whom I hoped this analysis would bring me closer. Who tells me, "Calm down, relax, take this ending in your stride".

And "Y" isn't great for my old friend with the flat, who like me grew up too soon, with whom I often discuss my analysis and who warns me of its dangers.

And then what am I to call Him, the analyst, about whom I wish to write in this diary? "Z"? Or "ZZZZ" more like, since he may well be dozing while I'm on the couch? Have to ponder further.

So what did ZZZZ say in the session yesterday?

Nothing.

What will he say in the session tomorrow?

Nothing.

What will he say in the session on Friday?

Nothing, I suppose.

Take some pleasure writing this, even if it's not quite true, since he does mutter the odd word and emit the occasional sound.

On several occasions during the course of 1995 I spoke to my analyst, ZZZZ, though always from supine on the couch, about my idea of ending the analysis, or interrupting it at least, come Christmas, with a view to escaping Paris to Italy for an eight-month sabbatical I'd been granted by the university where I teach. Would this, I asked him, be an opportune time or an appropriate stage? Surely on something as basic as this, and with which he presumably had a lot of experience, he must have some insights to offer. I didn't think it viable – this was my dig at him – that we continue the analysis on the telephone, despite the fact that given how little he had to say there wasn't much chance of our both speaking at once.

"No comment?" I asked him.

". . ."

Come September, it was my last chance to ask the university for a postponement of the sabbatical. But what had been one of the positive aspects of my idea, the linking of the end of analysis to an external event, had turned into a worry, that this ending lacked any sort of inner necessity. For all I knew, maybe this was just the *wrong* time to stop, I might be on the threshold of some big breakthrough, chrysalis into butterfly, larva into grub, dead flesh into dust – some such quaint metamorphosis. Given how few indications ZZZZ offered me as to where I was in my analysis – *few* is exaggerating, he offered me *no* indications whatsoever – then my worry was surely justified.

I decided to confront him and force him to spill the beans. (Ve have vays of making men talk.)

And so, one session in mid-September, after he pulls back the curtain and shows me through to the consulting-room, I don't make my usual way directly to the couch and stretch out. Which means that he, who never sits down in his armchair before I'm settled, remains standing, trying not to look surprised.

I plonk myself on the uncomfortable Louis-something chair where I squirmed my way through the early sessions some five and a half years before.

"I was wanting to ask you about my finishing here at the end of the year?" I try to add an inflection so this will come out sounding like a question.

"Hmmmm?" His is certainly a question.

"What do you think about it? I could always ask for a postponement on the sabbatical, but I'd have to ask now."

"Cchmmm."

"Are there some guidelines you can give?" I almost add "man to man", but in the context, where that "manhood" is more than a little in question, it might sound far-fetched. "Come on, you're the one with the experience. I've got only this analysis to judge from, which means I can't really judge at all."

"Ah yes?"

"I thought there might be some rules to this."

He raises his eyebrows – a reaction at last.

"And do you think," he starts, "do you really think that rules cannot be analysed?"

I sit there trying to take in his response. So he's saying I'm looking for a rule, trying to get him to lay down the law? Probably so as to kick it in the face once I've found it, that would be like me; trying, like some coach once said to the Scottish rugby team, to "get the retaliation in first".

"You're saying that what I'm asking is an *analytic* question, is that it?"

He only smiles, and gestures to the couch.

Curiously, I don't have to drag myself across the room, but even as I curse him under my breath for his unhelpfulness I stride forward and throw myself onto the couch with a sigh of relief. He's certainly a creep for not helping me. But at least he didn't fall into my trap.

Was I aware I was laying a trap?

Certainly not. But then that was probably because I was convinced that my ignorance would make the trap all the more enticing.

Wednesday 22 November

Walking down rue de Rivoli past the BHV department store on my way to analysis, plastic bags in hand, 2 children run past, 4 or 5 years old. Turn instinctively to watch them, jam my left foot in a hole in the pavement and twist my ankle – not bad enough to stop my dervish-whirling, but bad enough to make me wonder.

As predicted, ZZZZ his usual mute self today, despite my demands. Not a word on the pains of my current homelessness, and forget it for any offer of a comfortable place to stay. Not a word either on the related question of children, or how it bears upon my own proper name.

No luck there, so what about that other chestnut outstanding, also bearing upon proper names? Maybe thinking about it will help me ignore the chill in this ruin of my flat, and I'll delight over tonight's wisdoms whilst steaming in Y's bath tomorrow night after work.

Start at the beginning, with my own: "Dan Gunn". Only starting there is no start at all since, as I pointed out to ZZZZ today, my father got there before me, as he was "Gunn" and "Dan" too. What about "I", by which I usually refer to myself? Well, this barrage of words is coming out – "I" this, "I" that – as if I'd forgotten that so much of my analysis has been devoted to exploring how I feel betrayed by this pronoun which has already been used and abused by half the human race.

Is this "Dan Gunn" a real person upon whose analytic adventures a report can be directly issued? Or is he a figment remaining to be devised? Is he (am I) one with the biographical "Dan Gunn" who apparently holds a passport, appears in the telephone directory, has a job, writes books, inhabits a ruin? Reasonable questions. But questions to which the answers, unlike the name, aren't <u>given</u>. Questions to which analysis itself is supposed to provide answers. Is, to follow a well-worn formula, the resemblance to persons living or dead just coincidental or is it real and verifiable? At the risk of sounding glibly postmodern, I can only say: I wish to fuck I knew! Where I look for facts I find fictions. But when I to begin to spin tales, I stumble upon facts, the "givens" of my existence.

And by the way, did I say a <u>barrage</u> of words? The military metaphor is probably no accident for someone with a name like mine.

And the others?

Well, my old and loyal friends don't deserve to be tangled up in my mess any more than they already are just by knowing me. Hence "X". But can't I do better than that? How about, say . . . "Eve"?

Why "Eve"?

Because she tempted me? Because I'd like to be her first man? Because she's the night before a big day? Or because it makes her a palindrome, and recto—verso she is one and the same? That may well be it, for no one receives <u>a tergo</u> like she does. Though in some sense maybe it doesn't much matter what I call her, could be "Ethel" or "Morag". Though "Ethel" becomes "Ethereal" and "Morag" turns into "More-age". God, I'll be here all night if I go on like this. Maybe it's random, maybe necessary. For all I know the fiction may be closer to the truth than the fact. And I'll dispense other names too in this summary fashion, rechristening friends and colleagues alike, like some megalomaniac potentate, like a novelist. So "Y" becomes "Justine". That's a rich one, drawn straight from the Marquis de Sade whose books I'm teaching at the moment.

But that still leaves the question of ZZZZ. "The analyst" will sometimes do, even if it remains to be seen just how much, or more like how little, he has in fact analysed. How about a pseudonym? "Mr Shrinker"? "Dr Mirror"? Or abbreviate him to "Mr S." or "Dr M."? But by hanging a veil of anonymity, I'm giving the impression, first and foremost to myself, that behind this veil there lurks a real flesh-and-blood person with an identifiable, not revealable, proper name, and that this person is the secret repository of the truth. Curiosity directed thus towards what's hidden, what's biographical and individual. The sort of curiosity stimulated when some of the old stars of the couch are discovered, when Freud's famous "Wolf Man" is found to be still alive and howling. Off run the curious to find out "the truth", missing the point that if there is a truth in the psyche, it doesn't talk to hacks through some sort of confession. If the truth were that easy to tell, then we wouldn't need analysis (or fiction for that matter) in the first place.

(The thoughts are flowing, but I can't say I'm feeling any less cold. And I just heard a mouse scuttle through the ruins somewhere perilously close to my trouser-leg. Keep writing to keep awake.)

Names do matter, yes they do, and so do individuals and personal identities. But aren't names also stumbling blocks on the way to realities, words, beings, inventions, "truths" perhaps, which are imperturbably im_personal? These are free of my private pound of flesh and of the analyst's too. No veil, therefore, no pseudonym or abbreviation, no proto-Wolf Man. Write his name how it is. Focus attention on what's unknown to me and probably unknown to him as well. Focus attention on what remains to be discovered or imagined.

So: <u>Renato</u>.

It's no crock of gold, but at least it doesn't intimate that there's a crock which propriety is preventing me from sharing. Chuckle, recalling the occasion – I'd been seeing him for a couple of years, a period when I was longing to slough a skin, let go of tired old ways and become anew – here's me labouring forth with a boulder of guilt on my back worthy of Dante's Purgatorio Canto X, when I say to him: "I want to be replenished".

"Ah really!" An uncharacteristically generous intervention.

"I want to start again, be anew."

"So, you want to be Renato?"

It takes me a second or two, but I get there in the end: Renato–Reborn.

I laugh. The session's over.

As for Sergeant, his surname, no gift this either. Here's the Sergeant at Arms come to arrest me. Here's the foot-soldier plodding off to fight the war with his Gun(n). And here, just for me, is Lady Agnew of Lochnaw, staring out at me with her beautiful big dark eyes. Fancied her ever since I saw the portrait of her in the Scottish National Gallery, dressed in her diaphanous white gown with its flamboyant lilac sash. That look of hers, between defiance and entreaty, the left arm draped across the chair as if waiting for another hand to hold. And the whole portrait painted with an astonishing lack of inhibition by – John Singer Sargent.

There's a start: Renato Sergeant. Start of an end?

The mouse has gone to sleep. My turn now.

My father was a house-builder. While I, to judge from the ruins in which I currently found myself, with the shower-water pouring in from above and the rodents taking over, was no house-builder, still less home-maker. I was a Pyrrhus of home destruction.

"How on earth did you let this happen to you?" Justine asked me as she lent me the keys to her flat. "Doesn't your man have something to say about it?"

Didn't he?

I tried to be straight with myself, though I realised it should mortify me to admit it: my analyst's comments and interpretations over the six years, when his direct questions were excluded about specific words, names, facts which he wished to have repeated or confirmed, and the ritual "Good day", "Bonjour", "Goodbye", or "Au revoir" (which he tended to pronounce in the language corresponding to whatever I'd said first), and set aside too the odd discussion about holidays, rescheduled sessions and other organisational details – all this apart, and it doesn't amount to much, and everything he said, I mean the whole six years of his outdribblings, could be written down on a few pages of A4 paper, if written in a small hand. Legion, therefore, are the subjects on which he failed to pronounce – and if "failed" is too loaded, then "neglected", "omitted", or "declined". Few of which cut more deeply, from within the narrowing perspective of the end I was fast approaching, than his silence upon the question of my problem with houses, with homes, through which glowered my name, and its relation to my father and paternity. For had it not been what had driven me to his door in the first place?

It? My inability to build a home, a *foyer*, turn the generations, become a father. It was an *inability*, on another scale from the reluctance or doubt I witnessed in many males my age. The fact that I could spend happy evenings reading *House and Garden* or *Belles Demeures*, or that I adored having children round me, that when I first turned to the Sergeant I was in a stable relationship with a woman, Trinh, who knew she wanted one day to be a mother – all this exerted as much purchase on my inability as a wilted flower upon Sisyphus's boulder.

It wasn't as if I'd failed to work on the problem myself. Oh, the books I read, the theories I developed. Before I even properly understood that psychoanalysts were real people, who saw real patients, I was reading Carl Jung, then Wilhelm Reich, and when I tired of them I ploughed my way through the Pelican Freud Library, then through Winnicott. When I moved to France I was on to Jacques Lacan, and even his impenetrable style didn't put me off. All their famous notions, of archetypes, repression, screen-memory, dream displacement and condensation, Oedipus and Antigone, mirror and anal stages. Yes, I thrashed around with the machete of theory, and I actually imagined I was making some progress. But when I got to the clearing in the forest of my psyche, what did I see? Myself, in the midst of a ruin, with a child on my back like some incubus out of Fuseli who was about to cut my throat.

"Woh! Get down off there!" I shouted at it. "Put your cheese-wire away! My attempt to do up my flat has proved a fiasco. My contraceptive tyranny is so absolute, I've virtually tied a knot in my foreskin!"

Great idea I developed: being comfortable in a home and having a child would kill me, because it (therefore I) had somehow, magically, killed my own namesake father before me.

But however convincing the idea, all it amounted to was a second wilted flower to add to the first one, the pair of which I now applied to Sisyphus's stone. A child ran down the street and my head turned. I didn't expect by entering analysis to move from the utter interdiction upon paternity to being some sort of vizier or Mormon. I just wanted to be like other men, with the usual doubts and fears.

As I crept amongst the fallen plaster and flaking paint of my flat, with this one month of analysis to go, I saw that Sisyphus's boulder was still there, but that I'd dropped the wilted flowers. Eve never asked me for an Abel, so I never had to counter with a Cain. My contemporaries were wading through nappies, and others through legal suits to decide who would have the kids on which days. The children of even the least successful of them contained or emitted something marvellous. I was pleased that my old friend Matthew managed to have children despite his own doubts (doubts which stemmed from the bisexuality he was discovering at just the time, aged five, that I was getting to know him). Yet the road was blocked to my own *belle demeure*, nor could I find it in my heart to envy or pity parents.

The metaphoric boulder hadn't moved, only found its place amongst the not-at-all metaphoric rubble of my ruined flat.

"One thing at a time," Eve teased me. "First learn to love, then learn to give your sperm their teeth."

"Eh?" I asked the Sergeant. "So it's decided now that I'll never be at home, never be a father?"

"Hmmmm."

"Is that a question?

". . ."

Thursday 23 November

Almighty trek across the city with as many bags as I can carry, up the seven flights to Justine's one-room flat. At last settled sufficiently to wonder in disbelief: Can it really be 6 years since I started going to see the Sergeant, or more exactly 5 years 10 months? Verified it by looking into the journal I kept during the first months with him. At a frequency of 3 times a week (Tuesday, Wednesday, Friday) and 250 francs a session that makes a total cost I don't dare even begin to count up.

Had to search for that journal from the first months, under the piles of junk displaced from the bedroom into the sitting-room since the hopeless business of fixing up my flat began. Dipped into it, but it sure was tedious and tight-arsed. This time no such limits. Back then I convinced myself that it was better (better for whom?) if in my notes I transcribed nothing of what got said in the sessions themselves, just the setting, the events and details leading up to and away from the sessions. Why such strictures? Some idea of not dispersing myself, maybe? Keeping the words spoken in the session protected from the words written in the journal, and vice versa? Well, stuff that, I've no worries now about imposing limits. And as for dispersing myself, that would be just fine by me, an ideal promiscuity.

Pour in all three types of bubbly, get into the bath and soak, then finish off this entry submerged under a layer of thick white suds.

Made me wonder again, that journal: When I entered psychoanalysis, what exactly was I? In despair? Depressed? Short on hope or optimism? Or just anxious? Neurotic?

Not in despair exactly, but a bit of all the rest. Almost worse, with none of despair's colour or drama. Monochrome tastelessness. What else? Convinced of course I could never create a home, attempting to become a father would prove fatal, a death-threat connected to my failure to mourn my own father, died when I was five. All sorts of problems with endings. A fairly sophisticated set of physical, or more like psychosomatic symptoms, from sore throats to colitis, unresponsive to medical treatment, orthodox or alternative. Stuck in a rut, ancient at only 31, living my days under the pall of a grey Scottish Sunday reserved exclusively for acts of mercy and necessity. A modicum of public success – the post at the university in Paris, my writing being published, reviews for various newspapers and journals – but only serving to highlight, or further dim-light, the inner torpor.

Enough! Enough! Spare us the details!

Before analysis I was a bundle of aches and grumbles. Or at least, that's what I remember being. Only, what becomes of yesterday's aching toe or head, when today the pain has passed? The pain leaves its trace, but the memory of pain is nothing like a yelp or a moan. And psychoanalysis, more than other sorts of medical attention, puts this fact into relief.

Thinking back on the person I was when I started analysis, I'm doing so as the person I've become. The difference isn't just in what I'm thinking about but in the source of the thoughts, the person from whom the thoughts are emerging, in a mix of memory, fantasy, and forgetting. The past not stable but constantly rediscovered, even reinvented, by the present. Maybe it's only a slight exaggeration to say that I might best judge the ending fast coming upon me by how effectively I mis-remember the person I was, pains and all, six years ago!

The "person", I write, overstating my clarity. It's probably not by chance that when I stand up, I find myself covered in a thick white coat of bubbles.

Before I started psychoanalysis I wasn't aware of harbouring any special fondness for sheep, still less a fascination for them, and as for the idea that I might think of *myself* as a sheep, it had never even occurred to me. Yet now, with that analysis about to end, it was more than just the bubbles, more than the fact that Eve occasionally called me "lambkin", that made me ready to reaffirm my connection to that unspectacular and in so many ways unappealing species. Whoever's spent time on the Scottish hillsides will know I'm scarcely being ungenerous in my estimate: walk up to a sheep, and it will stare at you with eyes in which blind panic is vying with stupidity, before it hurtles itself into the nearest barbed-wire fence or peat bog, obliging you to spend the next half hour getting scratched or sodden trying to extricate it.

Notwithstanding the stupidity, however, or the panic-stricken eyes, the spindly legs or the apparently boundless lack of imagination, notwithstanding even the inability to keep the bottom clean, I found myself more and more preoccupied with sheep as my analysis progressed.

For "wool-gathering" the *Oxford English Dictionary* gives "the action of gathering fragments of wool torn from sheep by bushes, etc.". When for me psychoanalysis was such a "gathering" of the fragments of the self, of the tufts which had been snagged on various obstacles encountered during my life. "Wool-gathering", when during the final month of my analysis, just as I was hoping for some new clarity and sense of wholeness, what I was finding was that the obstacles were all the more prominent – versions of the barbed wire and the peat bogs – and that I seemed to be leaving fragments of myself all over the place. "Wool-gathering" too, probably, because in my journal I hoped again to gather myself together, this time not in words spoken but in words committed to paper. And, though this is an aspiration which I knew I couldn't realise alone, perhaps I hoped not just to collect the woollen fragments, but to spin and knit them too, into a garment to keep out the cold and be shared.

In addition to the literal definition, the dictionary gives the figurative sense of "wool-gathering": "purposeless thinking, wandering fancies", and so by extension "indulging in idle imagining".

("Keep your mind on the job!" Eve would admonish me, judging from my buttocks rather than from the bleary look in my eye.)

Anyone in any sort of therapy, with any sort of therapist, will experience a good deal of "purposeless thinking", even if not that more specialised type of wool-gathering particular to psychoanalysis, called "free association". Not that the questions patients ask themselves or their therapists will feel at any given moment to be idle or fanciful. The questions are more likely to feel pressing or crucial. Rather, even as a question is formulated, it may be sensed that there's no immediate answer. And there may be a more indistinct sense that the crucial question being formulated today, precisely because of the therapy and even if no answer is directly forthcoming, will by tomorrow merely raise an eyebrow or an amused smile. The question will glimmer in the distance already, seeming as "idle" as idle can be. Wool-gathering is an activity which can be directed not only towards what has already occurred, but also, through dream, fantasy, or fiction, towards the open future.

The dictionary adds a final definition, one which might seem diametrically opposed to what is so intensively cerebral an activity as psychotherapy or analysis: "being in an absent-minded state". Certainly, by entering analysis, I was obliged to concentrate my mind, and concentrate *upon* my mind. Yet experience showed just how inaccessible this mind was which I was trying so hard to concentrate, and more inaccessible still the mind *upon which* I wished to concentrate – so inaccessible as to be virtually "absent". It's not just that analysis made me feel much more blank and stupid. But I actually found myself elsewhere altogether, miles from anything I could possibly identify as my "mind" – even if, fortunately, not quite "out of my mind".

Friday 24 November

Always imagined, prior to analysis, that the further I go back, or down, or in, to my life, psyche, past, the more inevitably I'd find traces of my mother tongue. Hence the importance I attached to finding an analyst who spoke English and the hoops I made the French-Canadian Sergeant jump through when I first went to see him, checking on his vocabulary and comprehension. Experience has shown me the opposite is the case. Is that because I'm genuinely freer in French? Because foreign words stick easier to the foreign parts of my person? Or just because I know the Sergeant's French is better than his English?

The other day I wrote how I could be clear about the problems with my flat, that at least these were simple and pragmatic. Who was I trying to kid?

On the couch today amidst all my talk of collapsing walls and the water pouring in from upstairs, a sudden sense – when "sense" is the wrong word, implying meaning and direction – a sudden glimpse, like a bird's wing brushing past my face, and when I turn my head it's gone. A glimpse of having left behind every responsibility, imaginary or real. I'm immeasurably alone and free. Then the glimpse is gone. In its place stands a word. It tells me there's nothing simple about my flat and its problems.

The word is: <u>fuite</u>.

All the recent days, weeks, as if a whole lifetime, are suddenly crystallised in that single word.

"Me and my fuites!"

"Indeed!"

Seated here at Justine's table, I see even more clearly how that word gathers me up and welcomes me to vagrancy. Let me try and list its aspects.

1   A <u>leak</u> which trickles or bursts from a pipe, passes from one building into another. Leads to dampness, discomfort, accusations, recriminations. Requiring the Law, since, water being labile, precise causes for the discomfort are hard to ascertain, responsibilities hard to determine. Such as the one which has been spoiling my flat for ten years and which until very recently I half-heartedly endeavoured to have mended.

2   A <u>leak</u> that periodically affects my colon, then my sphincter. Never a good "eater", I refuse nourishment from the outset, recall being locked in the bathroom with the dinner to consume (probably fantasy, since the bathroom could be locked only from the inside). School meals a nightmare. Entero-Vioform an early companion, then Imodium and Spasfon. Stanched in late adolescence when I learn to cook, but back with a vengeance in late twenties, leading to endoscopy for a burning colon. Then, dramatically, all gone within the very first month of entering analysis. For five years barely a trace, until exactly one year ago, when it starts again, and lasts three months, thanks to Roberta. She empties me so thoroughly that I no longer know, inside-out as I've become, if I'm what is leaking or what has leaked.

(There's a third "leak" too, but this list risks falsifying not just the leaks themselves, but the whole analytic process. The three don't come serially, 1-2-3, though that would already be interesting. No, they come all together in an ungovernable unplanned lump, together because they <u>are</u> <u>one</u>, and this one is or <u>am</u> I. Better still, this one <u>would</u> <u>be</u> I, the I I'm still trying to become, to invent. This confluence is like the giddy moment before an uncontrollable belly-laugh. It's the moment when the mind can take no more and is set to lose itself, in which loss there's further gain. The mind relaxes its grip in favour of something so apparently animal and yet in fact uniquely human: laughter.)

3   An <u>escape</u> or <u>flight</u>, down all the routes I should have taken, leading I don't know whither, unless to that senseless sense of

freedom. Fuck the lot of them, whoever they are! I'm up, and out, I'm leaving behind even the loved ones – especially the loved ones. I've no idea where I'm going. But every time I feel the thrill inside me of something new and untried, like that first day of Scottish spring with all its promise, then I'm on that route. It leads away from my real life, in which I've heaped obligations, qualifications, duties, incumbents, upon my head, friends and colleagues too, only stopping short at a wife and kids.

"I can think of all sorts of ways of combining the three types of fuite," I inform the Sergeant, "though in fact it's more like pulling them apart since they're wrapped up together."

"Chhgmmm?" (How do I transcribe a clearing of the throat with a question-mark attached?)

"Any story I tell you, about one fuite causing another fuite, would be a poor show, compared with all three together. For example, that I have a flat which leaks which causes a body to leak because I didn't escape when I should have."

"Hmmmm?"

"And I'm escaping because I have a body which leaks, and it only leaks because my flat leaks. All the cause and effect, all the cart and horse and chronology are just a joke – or rather they're no joke, they're a kill-joy. The joke is that there's no chronology, causality or anything of the sort with its 'becauses' and 'therefores', they're just ways of stopping myself from laughing at the fuite which I am, have been, and forever more would become."

". . ."

"And I still can't believe you never helped me with Roberta. Of all the times you let me down, this is the most flagrant."

"Really?"

"You were jealous. Can't blame you for that. Her rosy ripe breasts and the Blairgowrie nipples – not that you've ever tasted a Blairgowrie raspberry, you poor fool."

"Hmm. Eh bien."

"Feeling the pinch, are you?"
And he's up, and I'm out.

Short dyed straw-yellow hair, thick myopic spectacles, a generous smile, joints made of rubber, and an acute version of that special way Italians have of relating to the ground, as if it were a deeply alien, even hostile surface – little wonder they're the greatest makers of shoes. That was Roberta. She would never have suggested it, I suppose, but when I called her up, she said, "Certo!"

It was November 1994, just around the time I was asking about my sabbatical, when I invited Roberta from Milan to the Valle d'Aosta, which I was visiting for my Toussaint holiday. We walked through the forests all afternoon, then spent the next twelve hours exhausting ourselves in experimental rejuvenating sex.

I intended this affair to be light and breezy, to help me forget how bogged down I was with Eve. Wanted to be flippant for once, stop being anxious and uptight. So when she took the train back to Milan the next evening, I told myself it was a good thing too.

Within a week I'd virtually ceased to sleep. I was lucky if I managed two hours a night, and then I'd dream of toilets, wake with a start, and check to see what time it was (as if it made any difference). Eating became a penance, since I'd no sooner down a mouthful than my guts would start aching. I called Roberta up and arranged to meet her some weeks later in London, when my teaching for the semester would be finished. When I got there I was exhausted from insomnia. I had to ask her not to lean too heavily on my distended stomach during some of her more gymnastic manoeuvres. And my time when not in bed was spent in the toilet, venting the diarrhoea which started then and persisted for the next twelve weeks.

I tormented the Sergeant with the details of our few days and nights together: the couplings, the condoms, her bendy-toy joints, the beauty of her breasts and the discretion of her rosebud.

"Your Cerutti seems to be pinching you a bit there," I'd tell him. "Down-under."

And I reminded him, one year on, insisting that though I didn't want to see Roberta again, I did want to see what had happened between us, and by seeing let go of her one final time.

So the leaves were falling in the Valle d'Aosta when I called Roberta up.

"Ciao," she said when she got off the train. "Ciao," she said when she got back on it eighteen hours later.

She wasn't there and then gone, I now realised, she was there and *already* gone. My delight was lived under the sign of an ending where the leaves would not be the only falling things.

"It's hardly surprising I became confused," I tell the Sergeant one year on. "Hardly surprising my insides tried to become my outsides. It was all over between us before we'd even started."

"Hmmm?"

I'd always known Roberta was intensely and systematically promiscuous. In addition to her official *fidanzato*, she had at least four barely less official lovers, as I'd learned from a friend who introduced me to her and who had been one of them many years before. Yet this hadn't put me off, on the contrary it had spurred me on. Was this because she was thus an easy channel through which to play out some homosexual fantasies, in that I would, by imagining her with these men, be taking pleasure for myself from these men? That would have been simple by comparison, and would have fitted well with the wish which was surfacing strongly in the last year of analysis, that the tedious bonds of gender be broken at last. But alas, nothing so neat.

"Dai tu, caro, io non posso godere."

Working back through schoolboy Latin, I finally got there. Non posso godére: No can joy.

Even in her ready availability Roberta remained profoundly unavailable; even as she was moving towards me, she was already moving away. Ciao ciao. And for the sake of this twisted farewell I'd done my damnedest to turn myself inside out, and occasionally back to front and upside down as well. The months of Roberta were the only time, I now realised, and would remain the only time, during which I was in what identified itself clearly as a "phase" or "stage" of analysis – *anal* of course, with all those dreams of toilets.

"I was drawn to Roberta," I inform the Sergeant, "like an infant to its *caca*. It's available, fun to play with, and somehow already there. But then from the moment you put your hands on it you've already lost it, you can't put it back where it came from, you find yourself covered in it, and the more you fidget the more you find yourself covered. When it's there it's gone. But if you keep hold of it then it's gone as well, even before it appears."

". . ."

"And if I see this a bit clearer now, then it's because of the contrast with here, with you. Not just because you don't have delightful breasts or bendy joints."

". . ."

"Roberta pluperfect. She had ever already left me. But between you and me – the contrast – nothing has yet been decided. If we've a tense, then it's the conditional, the tense of children's play, of fiction."

". . ."

I knew that if I kept my nerve, then in a month's time I would cease to see the Sergeant. Yet though the end was nigh, this didn't mean it was all over between us: I wasn't mourning in anticipation or stealing a march on time by pre-empting what time would throw up.

Bonjour . . . Au revoir.

He hadn't already left me, even if he was, in his own way, decidedly promiscuous, with all those patients of his.

My digestion went like clockwork. Not that there wasn't still plenty of confusion or *confluence* – those *fuites*. But all was yet to play for. Through his high-risk strategy of refusing interpretation of my back-to-front infatuation, the Sergeant kept the mystery alive of what comes first, what last. He allowed me the better to find Roberta, the better to lose her.

As I walked towards the métro during these November days I kicked the last piles of autumn leaves, blessing my every *fuite*.

Saturday 25 November

In the year of Our Lord 1963 I quietly closed the front door behind me and set out for I knew not where. I was five years old. My father had died the night before, the father to whom I had until then been linked by an almost Siamese bond, and who, as I was only beginning to realise, had, by his sudden massive heart attack, offered me a gift beyond reckoning, a prize untold.

"You will have to be brave," my mother told me.

I was squirming on her knees, intimidated by all the men in their dark suits who were staring at her, at me, or out of the window, in embarrassment.

"You will have to be brave because your father is dead."

I jumped off her knees, despite her protestations – she wanted me to stay, feel the drip drop of her tears on my scalp, stay with her, my elder brothers, and the suited men, doubtless wanted to comfort and console me, little guessing that I was already, in an instant, beyond all comfort and consolation, or they beyond me, that what I could not receive, neither could I give. I was no cushion or handkerchief or comforter. I had to be up and out, on my way, though I little knew whither.

Stepping into the hall, I was aware, momentarily, of my meagre five years. I tried to calculate how much younger I was than David Balfour when he sets out on his adventure (my father had been reading to me from Kidnapped the night before), but then remembered that I hadn't yet learned how to subtract. All my life I had scarce spent more than a few minutes alone, following my father on his daily round, in his Jaguar car, scrambling behind him as he strode across his building sites dispensing advice to his joiners and bricklayers.

Yet I was aware too that if I tarried longer amidst the suited men and the sobbing relatives, I might never escape, and that I should have to inhale their misery, which would rapidly fill my lungs such that they could never expel it fully. Oh, not in these words, of course, did my awareness announce itself — I was only five, and could not have told my lungs from my larynx. I only knew that I was suffocating, had to open the door and run.

"Where are you going?" my mother asked me.

I did not reply, only smiled to her. Should I take my pet hamster or my favourite pieces of Lego? I feared they would make me conspicuous. I opened the front door quietly, wondering if my father was upstairs, perhaps, in his coffin. Then I went out, and closed the door behind me.

I do not say I was <u>free</u>, for what would that mean. But I was <u>out</u> and I was <u>away</u>, and would evermore be further. I started to run, then had to stop because I couldn't breathe while I was chuckling — yes, chuckling.

And that laughter which shook me then has never quite ceased, so I only have to think of that day again to feel its tickle in the cheeks and lungs, where it filled the space of the misery my relatives were trying to breathe into me. Its sound is like autumn leaves rustling, like a pine cone racing, inhuman, shameless, and impersonal, across the frozen surface of Loch Awe.

When I scribbled down in my journal these lines about escape, my *fuite* from the house of grief, I genuinely thought I'd be able to develop them into a story. A journey, some picaresque adventure to convey the perilous course I did not take as a child, with its wild elation and erratic course the very opposite of the duty and guilt I contracted, and which had been instrumental in turning me to analysis nearly three decades later.

But as I tried to envisage the sequel, I realised that as soon as my boy protagonist were to determine a direction in which to flee, he'd become a prisoner to that, to his own new story, to forces which might well prove even more constraining than what David Balfour suffers when he's kidnapped and thrown into the hold of a ship, or when he's baked on a hot rock in the Highland sun. My young protagonist wouldn't escape, and I had not escaped either.

When I started analysis I didn't exactly expect to gain a new improved understanding of myself. Fortunately, since, as with my attempts to get off the potty with Roberta, I was usually led to confound contraries and chronology and often ended up with an almost indescribable compound of simultaneity and synonyms. I was bored with the books of theory I'd read and with the pet notions I'd developed on myself. The idea that the dark subterranean land of the unconscious, what Freud describes, borrowing the term from Virgil for his epigraph to *The Interpretation of Dreams*, as the "Acheronta", or "Infernal regions" – the idea that these regions would yield up their monsters and grotesques seemed to me pretty improbable, even undesirable. They'd only send up their simulacra or spies, while they dug their nails in deeper.

What I wanted was to change, cease repeating, find new words, ways of being, doing, inventing, to feel that freedom I tried to describe in the opening lines of my story. I wanted to see the world anew, as distinct from myself, and see it clearly, yes see *it* more than see myself.

There's a definition given by Jacques Lacan about the goal of analysis, and it lodged in my mind as surprisingly modest for a man so wildly immodest. That the patient starts an analysis by speaking to himself; goes on to speak to the analyst but about one who is not himself; but that when he will have spoken to the analyst about himself – who will have changed in the interim by this very fact – then the analysis will be over.

Only, I'd found something I wished to add to Lacan's modest proposal, a gloss upon that notion of change which goes with speaking of oneself, something thrown into relief by the last of the strange and paradoxical charms of playing bendy-toys with Roberta.

For to speak in and of one's own person, one would, I realised, have to speak in a new or foreign language.

What is it that, as much as all the rest, made my few days with Roberta so exciting and disturbing? The fact that, from the very first phone call I made to her, inviting her to the autumnal Valle d'Aosta, I was speaking a language – Italian – which I *did not know*. By which I don't mean one I didn't know I knew, but one I knew I didn't know.

Here's me picking up the phone, speaking whole sentences of invitation, when up until then my Italian has consisted of a few stumbling words. And when we meet, I spend a whole day conversing with words, phrases, expressions over which I have only the flimsiest control. This is nothing like my English, obviously, which I've been hearing from birth, nor like my French, which is forever tainted with memories of school, and which by the time I got to France had lost its foreign feel. No, words are streaming out of my mouth which I have no recollection of ever having heard before.

The cabin in Valle d'Aosta has only one single bed. Roberta offers to share it with me, though no private words have yet passed between us. I sit nervously on the bed next to her. Here goes, I think, as I try to utter.

"Cosí," I stammer, "dormiamo insieme."

She looks at me, eyes wide.

"*Anzi*, facciamo l'amore!"

She fails to suppress a giggle.

It is of course a ridiculous thing to say. Something like: "So we're sleeping together – *what is more/or rather* let's make love!"

Yet it works. And even if she'd said, "No, get off me you illiterate creep" (or some Italian version thereof), it would still have been a success, since for the very first time I use that tricky word "anzi".

Anyone who's learned a foreign language, especially when grown up, will know something of this thrill. Here's lust walking in step with intelligence, that's a rare and exhilarating thing. But here too is language, and it's speaking all by itself!

To end analysis, one year on, to end it *well*, I decided, would be to speak in such a language, or be spoken by it, in a manner both completely personal and deeply impersonal.

In the case of a foreign language this thrill cannot last, and the way Roberta faded from my life was no doubt connected to my increasing familiarity, developing into *knowledge*, of the Italian language. Somewhere else, when defining the goal not of analysis but of love, the same Lacan picks up on one of Plato's definitions, and renders it as "giving what one does not have". With Roberta, briefly, I "spoke a language I did not have".

To end analysis, I told the Sergeant, would be to speak to him of me in just such a language. That word *fuite* was one of the first words to note in the lexicon of this new language. It allowed me, if not to escape when I was a child, then to *imagine* what it was to escape, even way back then. And that imagining was *already* an escape.

And every time I do more than sip the tepid tea of jaded pleasures, feel the stir inside, imagine writing a new book, touching a new woman, sleeping under an olive tree on a Tuscan summer night, or reaching the peak of Ben Lomond on a frost-bound winter's morn, think of Proust or *The Odyssey* (think of the books which, like all great books, make me feel new again and free), it's not just the legacy of loss which I'm feeling. It's also the distant echo of those heartfelt words that may or may not have been mine as a child of five, even if the voice and terms are clearly adult – "Fuck the lot of you, I'm off!"

For which words I now thanked my father.

And for which I thanked the Sergeant as well?

That remained to be seen. For would I ever really leave him? Would he be behind me, calling me back, or be turned away in anger or indifference, shaking the hand of my successor? Would his door stay open as I left, or would it be slammed shut and firmly bolted?

Sunday 26 November

Where on earth did I think I'd find time to write the sequel to those pages of the boy's adventure, even if I had been able to find some directionless direction for him to take?

Ridiculous idea even without the public transport strikes which have started. They're going to make travel across the city a nightmare. I'm a past-master at finding the few métro lines still operating and jumping from one to another. But this time it promises to be different. It may even outfox an experienced métro-hopper like myself. I can't even get in to the stations, walked from porte de Bagnolet to Père-Lachaise, and they were all locked up. Not a bus in sight. Yet somehow I have to get from Justine's flat in the extreme east of the city to my building site in the north, then down to work at the university in the south-west. And back. Five days a week. Calculate it will take me about 3½ hours walking, each way. And meanwhile I've ambitions to write a story with no storyline, some adventure that will capture the thrill of a 5-year-old vagabond. That'll be right: tie a lectern to my chest and I'll write it while I stride the streets. Pah! All around me conspiring to make this ending anything but tranquil, and to deprive me of the space or time to figure out what it all might mean.

Including my dreams. What a mess! Not in the least like someone about to end an analysis. More like someone just beginning.

Last night: The water bursting through the ceiling of my flat, but I'm enjoying it. So much of it that it forms a pool, and I realise I'll have to swim across it, fully dressed (in the clothes I was wearing at my last session, Friday). Jump into the pool and try to swim, but it's far from easy. On the far side, who's that? Hah! It must be my father since I can't see his face, and that's probably my mother beside him. He's holding aloft a trophy which will be mine if I can only reach the other side. Realising which, I jerk awake.

If I wait till Tuesday to do something with this dream then it'll be cluttered under more than 2 days' junk by then. So I should try to make something of it alone: given 6 years' experience, surely I can get some way by myself. Given how little the Sergeant says, there may not be much difference between trying alone or in his presence.

So here goes.

Well, that was certainly some leak. Taking a leak, of course. And then, speaking of escapes, maybe I've gone back some way, since that pool, if I speak it as to the Sergeant, the pool may be a bassin, when bassin also means "pelvic floor".

Wonder why I swam across the amniotic pool fully dressed? Fully dressed for analysis, maybe. Which means to say that it's with Renato Reborn that this new birth is going to happen?

Hmmph! (I can even do my own Sergeant-impersonations.)

And on the other side, this figure of the father waiting to reward me as I emerge from the bassin. One of the biggest disappointments of analysis is that I can't see his face nor any other image of him. Not a single word of what he must have told me. Hoping none the less that in these last weeks my dreams will compile a "Best of" Album, with all my favourite themes and tracks. Since the Sergeant's so unwilling to sum up, it'll be handy if my dreams do it for me.

Not much point in hoping. Get on the phone, rather, and ask if I can borrow Justine's tiny bicycle for tomorrow.

"He'll surely talk you through it," Justine told me when she called back to check I was remembering to water her plants.

"I don't know about that," I said.

"Are you leaving him, or is he getting rid of you?"

It wasn't just because I knew Justine to have her own complex feelings about analysts and endings that I was at a loss for an answer.

"Anyway, he'll surely not just drop you with a bang, he'll reduce the frequency of sessions or something."

"Diminuendo?"

"Yeh, and don't forget that the yucca needs some talking to as well."

When I'd hung up and had time to think, I figured that Justine was surely right: diminuendo towards a restful silence into which I'd feel confident to step alone. That would be the sane way.

Whereas the reality was that my analysis seemed to be taking place on another plane altogether – another planet. Given all the Sergeant's grunts and sighs, why not Planet of the Apes. He was reluctant to "talk me through" anything whatsoever, and I was being reminded of this fact whenever I awoke to the sight of another triptych.

"Go on," I told him. "Look, if you can't get my dreams straight, then what chance for the rest?"

There's a popular view of dreams, a view that psychoanalytic writings often support, that dreams are puzzles or rebuses. In six years I'd done nothing more than scan the odd psychoanalytic text, since the desire to do so abandoned me when first I opened the Sergeant's door and started to speak. Yet I hadn't forgotten the delight, not dissimilar to that offered by a detective story, of reading Freud's accounts of dreams, his own and his patients', in *The Interpretation of Dreams*. By undoing the "dream-work", he tracked the "dream-wish" back to its lair and obliged it to speak its truth. Freud's notion that, however provocative, obscure, or disturbing the dream, it does contain a wish, expressed in the form of a puzzle, is indeed seductive, and at base reassuring.

Yet what I was finding, by contrast – and here's the link to Justine's doubts about my ending – was that within the puzzle, within each piece of the puzzle, there was another puzzle. The further I followed this sequence of puzzles, the less reassuring and more strange and surprising and beautiful each piece or puzzle became. Or, in short, there was no end to puzzling, unless imposed arbitrarily, violently, from somewhere outside the puzzle.

There's a wonderful scene in that most dream-like and hilarious of novels, Flann O'Brien's *The Third Policeman*, when Policeman MacCruiskeen reveals to the narrator a beautifully intricate chest which it has taken him two years to carve. The chest is so perfect that the Policeman can't think of anything worthy to put inside it. So what does he do? He carves another, identical, but slightly smaller chest and puts that inside, within that another, and so on. Intending to impress the novel's narrator, he takes out the first thirteen of the chests and arrays them on the table before him. The Policeman asks for a pin, and with its help, and a huge magnifying glass, he pulls out another twenty chests, the last few of which are "nearly as small as nothing".

Dreams and their puzzles are more like this than like Freudian detective stories, at least *my* dreams and *their* puzzles.

And what happens to the Policeman's precious chests? A clumsy man called Gilhaney comes into the station. Not noticing the invisible chests, he stumbles, and knocks them to the floor. One person's handiwork is another person's dust.

Dreams helped me to get going in the sessions, and a high percentage of my six years was spent recounting their twists and turns, since on the nights before my sessions I would often have not just one dream I recalled vividly, but two or three, what I called my "diptychs" and "triptychs". But ask an adolescent who's just awoken from a wet dream, and he'll tell you: there's a gap between a dream and anything it can be turned into as wide as between an explanation and a nocturnal emission. The dream contains resources of pleasure and proprioception of which one can only, in fact . . . *dream*.

Nothing gave me as many ready words as my dreams. Nothing confirmed the power of these words, but also their limitations, quite so strongly. Very simply: one can solve the puzzle, find the truth about one's dreams; but never the last and most intriguing puzzle. Never can one see the smallest and most beautifully intricate chest, never find or tell the *whole truth*.

What if the Sergeant led me, as Justine intimated he should, through a diminuendo, into a less-than-brutal close? Wouldn't that diminuendo be a bit like MacCruiskeen's chests? Even if he took me to silence or invisibility, it seemed there would still be plenty more to say, more chests to open, maybe the most important and fascinating of all. Not once did he raise the subject of my ending, let alone "talk me through it". But then – the connection – nor did he ever interpret a single one of my dreams, in the sense of giving them a meaning, cracking the code or puzzle, doing more than ask for a detail here or a highlight there. Never once a full-blown interpretation.

Of course this drove me, at times literally, to distraction. "Come on, you've got to have some idea!"

Never did he say anything to stop the flow, the stories, their proliferation and permutation.

However, he did act like Gilhaney and regularly knocked my chests to the ground. I'd be blethering on about some sexy complex dream – and sometimes I'd really only just started – when he'd rise to his feet to announce the session was over.

"Fill the Louvre with your diptychs and triptychs," he seemed to be saying, by his reluctance to interpret and his interruption of the sessions, "and still you won't make a likeness of yourself."

Or again, in the context of the ending fast approaching: "Blah blah blah, you can talk talk talk, and you'll never get it all said. If you're looking for closure, you're going to have to do a Gilhaney yourself, be violent or clumsy."

Monday 27 November (6.30 a.m.)

In little over half an hour I have to get on Justine's bike, remember how to cycle (I've always been too scared to dare cycling in Paris), and somehow defeat the gridlocked traffic to get to my own flat, where, amidst the rubble, I'm to act like a grown-up aggrieved citizen in front of lawyers and insurance men.

But first, my diptych (unless it has four parts?).

Panel 1:   I'm in an unfamiliar room with Eve, there's some unknown couple there too, and we're preparing for an orgy, all members (!) being consenting adults. Eve and I undress, she lies upon a table, parts her legs for me. (And even as I write this I feel myself stiffen — I'll be outdoing T.S. Eliot's Gerontion next, "when I / Stiffen in a rented house".) I busy myself with wondering how the second woman can add to my titillation. Look down to check I'm ready for imminent entry, then stare in disbelief, turning to delight, at my penis, which has become transparent. Not invisible, mind, but transparent, as if made of glass.

No time to think, in any case, since we're accelerated into a second dream-phase. I look up and round, but no one seems to have noticed my metamorphosis, though I believe it's the eighth wonder of the world. They're all impatient 'cos I'm not getting on with it. I look down, and what's happened this time? Jesus, it's returned to flesh and blood, but a worrying swelling on its right side. (In French that would be "côté droit", which sounds like "on the side of the law".) Finger it gingerly, spongy to touch. The swelling grows into a second organ, attached to the first. Has a vein burst? Two little flaps of liver-coloured skin which I can feel solely with my finger. Is this new organ mine? A sensation so upsetting that I awake with a fright.

Panel 2:   I'm walking through a port with Eve. French pronunciation could make the "port" a <u>porc</u> or "pig". But it's no pig, it's an enormous cow, waiting to be cut up. "Dismembered"? This cow belongs to me, as do the pieces it will become. Hope the butcher knows his business. But even as I look at it, it swells into an obscenely bloated corpse. I hurry on round a corner, hoping to leave the monstrosity behind.

But only to run into worse in phase two. Strewn on the ground are the remains of a goat which has already been cut up. Unbearable stench of piss, the pieces all micturated yellow. Blench and chunder! Run through the pieces, knowing that this smell will never leave me. With which knowledge I awaken.

Get dressed now and out to meet with my ruins and the Law.

Is it this sense, or senselessness, of inexhaustibility in the puzzle or tale, and the violence of any attempt at closure, that made me sceptical concerning what Justine said about "talking me through it"? The trouble being that I hadn't just become sceptical about this particular ending. No, the scepticism had spread to infect just about everything I touched.

There's a book by the literary critic Frank Kermode with the marvellous title, *The Sense of an Ending*. Not surprisingly, when searching for that sense, he turns back to the authority of scripture, and to God's hand running the show – such a god as would be able to see even the tiniest of MacCruiskeen's chests. Lacking such divinity, I would pick up a "well-rounded" novel, such novels as I used to enjoy before I started with the Sergeant, and even when they didn't finish pat with "And Reader, I married him", all I could feel was the factitious urge to get to a conclusion and sew matters up.

When the novel wasn't dropping from my hands, it was being thrown across the room in irritation.

Eve would laugh and suggest I try some dance steps instead.

There were exceptions, and with these I got on even better than before: Proust, for example, or Kafka, or Samuel Beckett.

But then these three writers had enormous difficulties imposing endings on their works, or forged their works from the extreme difficulty of ending. If their characters rush around, plot, scheme, plan, or just stand around and wait, it may well be because they're aware that ending or closure has become implausible if not impossible.

Not that I didn't *wish* to enjoy some of those well-rounded novels that had enchanted me before. I wished to (or wished to wish to), as I wished my analyst would solve my puzzles, interpret my dreams, and "talk me through" or at least "up to" the ending fast approaching. Oh I wished it all right, with more than a trace of the longing that drives Joseph K in *The Trial* to get into the High Court, or the doggedness which keeps Vladimir and Estragon returning to the same spot each day in the hope that Godot will arrive.

"You're a cruel sod," I told the Sergeant. "Incompetent and cruel."

"..."

And then?

Then I went on talking, dreaming, puzzling, re-reading the writers who still spoke to me. Then I went on writing too, in my journal.

Would there always be something more to say?

Trying to divide the delight of this from its attendant frustration was like trying to divide BRIGHTON from its rock. There was delight that some of my superstitions had lost their grip, especially those clinging to writing (adult versions of the gonks on the schoolboy's desk). I no longer felt secretive about writing, could move around with my pen and paper, and would set out on a story or article without a clue where I was heading. Yet there was frustration too that however many superstitions I'd lost or strictures I'd relaxed, I'd never been able, either in analysis or on paper, to get the whole story told, to express myself fully, to put my heart on my sleeve and let it be admired.

Eve didn't know a thing about my journal, but she guessed my general intention. As was her wont, she put it irritatingly well.

"You think," she said, "that you've found a shortcut to conveying the truth about yourself? Getting very Californian in your old age. 'I'm telling the truth, look I'm laying myself bare,' – that's you talking – 'and it must be true because I've paid all this money to an analyst to prove it'."

"Ho ho ho," I muttered, licking my wound.

I was thinking: If there's nothing natural about speech in the first place, still less anything natural about analysis or writing, then where does this leave that strange sort of supplement that is writing about analysis? The highly artificial mechanisms are obvious enough when analysts write, since it's so patent that they're doing so under duress, manufacturing scant scraps of knowledge they can share so as to relieve the diabolical solitude of their profession.

But their patients?

Despite what Eve said, I wasn't feeling much confidence in straight confession or autobiography. I wasn't about to go New Age and claim, either in analysis or on paper, that I was being honest or sincere. The easing of a few fears about giving myself away – fears that I'd have nothing left to give – didn't mean that giving myself away had become any easier. Not least when the scoundrel to whom I was seeking to give myself, during these final pressured weeks, refused to speak up and say, "That's it, I've got it. Now you've really given yourself away this time!"

Monday 27 November
(contd, 8.30 a.m.)

Forgot I'd have to pump up the tyres on Justine's bike, which meant finding a pump first. Last thing a man with dreams about bloated cows on his mind needs to be looking for. Then had to dash, cycling most of the way on the pavements since every inch of road was taken up by the stationary traffic. At least the fumes helped me forget the stench of that slaughtered goat.

Must have had Jo on my mind since as soon as I get into the

ruin, my eyes seek him out. Time maybe before they all arrive to jot down some of him:

> And it came to pass at the end of two full years, that Pharaoh dreamed: and, behold, he stood by the river.
>
> And, behold, there came up out of the river seven well favoured kine and fatfleshed; and they fed in a meadow.
>
> And, behold, seven other kine came up after them out of the river, ill favoured and leanfleshed; and stood by the other kine upon the brink of the river.
>
> And the ill favoured and leanfleshed kine did eat up the seven well favoured and fat kine. So Pharaoh awoke.
>
> And he slept and dreamed the second time: and, behold, seven ears of corn came up upon one stalk, rank and good.
>
> And, behold, seven thin ears and blasted with the east wind sprang up after them.
>
> And the seven thin ears devoured the seven rank and full ears. And Pharaoh awoke, and, behold, it was a dream.
>
> And it came to pass in the morning that his spirit was troubled; and he sent and called for all the magicians of Egypt, and all the wise men thereof: and Pharaoh told them his dream; but there was none that could interpret them unto Pharaoh.
>
> Genesis 41:1–8

Damn it! There's the first of them at the door. Haven't even got to Jo yet.

❖

"What about Joseph?" I'd ask the Sergeant. "Remember him?"
"Hmmmm."
"So?"

The less time I had left, the stronger was my desire to have Joseph reach out his hand to me, as he had when I was a child – maybe it was Joseph who was responsible for the couch thirty years later. The less time I had, the stronger my desire to hold solutions in my hand as I approached the gates of sleep each night. They'd be as satisfying, if not as cataclysmic, as the tale of kine and corn.

Yes, I did want to turn my dream-life into narrative, and for this narrative to have a satisfying ending, kine into corn into years, worms into cows into goats. And if the narrative had a moral twist, or an allegorical turn, then so much the better. Oh I wanted it all right, and sometimes I almost got it. But in the end there was no end: the more powerful my own interpretations – and as for the Sergeant's, forget it! – the more the dreams just generated further new stories.

I was busy in my analysis not assembling the jigsaw but pulling it apart. The more I spoke, the more I found myself not with a completed picture like on the box, as it might be of the Yalta Summit, or the map of Africa (the "Jig-Maps" I liked as a child). Rather I'd find myself with an odd piece, the tip of Churchill's cigar, or the name "Burkina Faso", in my hand, a piece which, once I'd held it in my hand long enough to describe it, had changed, slid, swelled, so it'd no longer fit back in the puzzle. See! Cigars, swelling; *book-in-a-face-oh*. And so I stared at the puzzle piece and tried to imagine what jigsaw might accommodate it, thinking jigsaw, thinking "I saw jig-jig"; indulging in what is called, quite wrong-headedly, "free association".

Wrong-headedly, for one is not in any real sense free, one does not choose the piece one holds in one's hand or the way it metamorphoses or the words this metamorphosis produces. Or if one does, then one doesn't recognise that "one" as oneself, and so *one* is, or are *two*, often more.

On Eve's desk, placed where I couldn't miss it, was a reproduction of a painting which she cut out from a magazine. I wondered if the Musée d'Orsay would have the nerve to make a jigsaw out of this startling image of a woman's naked crotch seen from below.

"L'Origine du Monde," Eve told me when she saw me staring, entranced. "By Gustave Courbet."

"This meant to be a turn-on?"

"Do you know who owned it?" she asked. "That's why I cut it out."

"I thought it belonged to the Musée d'Orsay."

"Before that?"

I had a queasy feeling.

"It says here that the museum bought it from one Jacques Lacan, or from his estate."

Queasier and queasier.

Can you imagine what it cost? How many people would have to, eh, contribute? I hope he let them stare at it at least as they were racing on and off his couch.

Queasier and queasiest.

For she was right, of course. Analysis isn't free, and association isn't free either, because, quite simply, you pay and pay. I had to make a conscious effort to dismiss the fact that I could now calculate just how much my entire analysis would have cost me. You pay and pay, *through the nose* you could say, but for the fact that noses are as bad as cigars in the way they grow, fall off (and it didn't take Freud to show us, Laurence Sterne devotes whole chapters of *Tristram Shandy* to noses). But for the fact that, as analysis was showing, when one says "You could say, but for", you're in fact already saying it, even if you're hiding it, removing the piece while pretending to leave it in place, having your cake and eating it.

*Un*free *dis*association. The image comes apart, and the sliding doesn't stop, often reaching crazy variegation, with an overdose of inconsistencies, paradoxes, incompatibilities, anachronisms, simultaneities, heterodoxies, and a random dissolution. And at the end, if there ever is one? At the end all that remains, if you're lucky, is something that resists all words, a residue that refuses to be translated.

A heather-clad hill on my right, and on my left a view to the sea. A burn flowing through a glen, and in the distance, high, a scree-slope, across which are moving, as I hood my eyes with my hand, some small white forms. It's a place with no precise proper name, and its elements can vary: a loch behind me, the sun turns to drizzle, or the heather becomes bracken, though the white forms remain. Yet it's always mysterious, beautiful, somewhat melancholy, and it's always unmistakably somewhere in Scotland, my homeland. Landscapes of which I dream regularly, and with such intensity that I awake with tears in my eyes and an incongruous smile on my face.

I suspect that for each person this dream-residue differs. Mine became clear over the years, and as the number of dreams I could produce for analysis became finite (even if I managed a triptych every night), I longed more and more to wander there, in that residue.

Here was the exception that proved the rule of disassociation and metamorphosis. For however often and insistently I spoke to the Sergeant of my landscape dreams, from which plot or narrative was always absent, I did not find the scenery slipping and dissolving into something other than itself. Of course, I could elaborate a fantasy or two, even without the help of all that rutting in the heather in *Rob Roy* or the paggering in *Braveheart* (I ordered the Sergeant to see them). And then maybe my words slid off the landscapes because, though I knew the Sergeant was Canadian, he now had such a bourgeois urban lifestyle that the most natural thing he encountered was the river Seine, with the occasional dead dog floating down it. But however hard I tried to incorporate the landscapes into my fantasies, or to appeal to whatever was left in him of the lumberjack, the bracken and heather only rustled in the breeze, the burn continued to flow, the clouds gathered over the peaks. The white forms just stopped for a second, then continued on their way, indifferent and unflustered, not changing or signifying, unless in ways quite unconnected to me and my presence.

This residue may have been lithographed upon the autochthonous memory-bank of my family and ancestors. Maybe it was handed down with my mother's milk. Whatever, the residue welcomed me while ignoring me utterly. It was a source of frustration, in that I was convinced my descriptions of it were failing to communicate its magic. But it was also the place where I really wanted to be, or where a part of me already was.

I rediscovered it, my analysis singled it out, dusted off the cobwebs, the words, the anthropomorphic images – the cigars, the jigsaws, and Joseph's helping hand. The heather bells ring more violet, the scree-slope glitters more greyly, and the white forms resume their pacing more inscrutably than ever.

Monday 27 November
(contd, 11.30 p.m.)

Fifteen men squeezed into my ruin of a flat, but no sign of a dead man's chest, and certainly no bottle of rum. Who are they all? Lawyers, insurance folk – but the rest? Passers-by who've come up for the fun? Fifteen men and one solitary woman.

Successfully feign outrage at how I've been unhoused, the final indignity after years of being leaked upon. And somehow, in the manufactured heat of my tirade, find the French terms for all my gradations of discomfort. (The "Expert" from the "Tribunal de Grand Instance de Paris" takes notes.) I'm outraged all right, only at this precise moment I'm more concerned with all the memories flooding back from being on a bicycle. And why is it I find that one woman so alluring?

Her presence is bound to be a relief amongst all that serious serge and pinstripe. She's also rather beautiful, tall, elegantly dressed. But there's more. I have to wait till the meeting's over (inconclusively of course – another meeting to be scheduled) to begin figuring out the remainder.

Her name: "Gobillot". Pretty close to the name of the lawyer played by Jean Gabin in that wonderful 1950s film, En cas de malheur, in which he's seduced by Brigitte Bardot. That splendid shot of B.B. from the side, leaning on his desk with her skirt hitched up.

40

Then the name of her company: "Cabinet Goldberg". Gives me a kick up the pleasure-nodes. For Goldbergs was the poshest department store in Edinburgh when I was a child – so it seemed to me – with the first automatic doors I'd ever walked through. My mother would take me there on her shopping trips. All those women's clothes, handbags, perfumes, and maybe some exotic Jewish presence. And as reward for my patience – little did she know how much I'd been enjoying myself – hot muffins with melting butter, up on the 6th floor, with a view over the city.

Finally, best of all, her title: "Maître". When one addresses her, it's not "Madame Gobillot", but "Maître Gobillot", or even just "Maître" tout court. "Oui, Maître", "Non, Maître". Like so many appurtenances of the Law, wildly erotic, even leaving aside the inevitable schoolboy memories of being beaten by my schoolmasters (French pornographers call it "éducation anglaise" – why not écossaise?).

I listen to that word Maître as it resounds, gendered and yet genderless, and masturbate to its ring – successfully too for the first time in months.

Merci, Maître!

Dreams taught me, dreams frustrated and puzzled me, dreams returned me to my heartland. But no single dream came close to the one that first announced farewell. This was the Verdi and Wagner of dreams, quite the most overwhelming I've ever experienced.

It happened in March, shortly after I told the Sergeant that my application for sabbatical had been accepted. How to convey the hyper-reality of what I lived that night, the lifetime of hope, folly, sadness, disgust, concentrated into a few hours or minutes? It opened some chamber within me, like the inner ear upon which we depend for equilibrium. Ever since then, new things have become audible, even though it also means that sometimes I reverberate and boom, at other times lose my balance and fall down.

In this dream I'm lying on the Sergeant's couch, with him behind me. I turn to him and realise I've received his permission to stay the night. What a bliss of belonging, with him watching over me.

I fall asleep, then wake, turn round, but he's still there, in his pyjamas now. "Aren't you cold?" he asks me.

When I nod, he takes a coverlet and puts it over me. Sleep again and wake again, turn, and this time he has dozed off, and a blanket is falling from his shoulder. He starts, caught napping, smiles to me reassuringly, as if to say, "The night is long, but we'll get through it together."

Then, just as I'm dropping off again, the door opens abruptly, and, to his immense embarrassment, in walks his wife. (And yes, he does have a wife, whom I occasionally cross on the stair, who receives clients of some sort in the room next to his.) She's dressed in an idiot's sackcloth smock, with long tasselled arms with which she can be pinioned.

I'm outraged at the intrusion, but this is nothing. She walks up to the couch, lifts her smock, raises a plastic bowl, and pisses into it, man's style. Then she tosses the bowl aside – not in my direction, thank God! – goes up to her husband who's now staring at her forbiddingly and shouting, "Stop it! Get back to your room!". She doesn't appear even to hear him, for she is – and I know this with a bone-crushing certainty – stark-raving mad. She falls to her knees, gropes for his fly, slips out his penis, which tumefies despite his best endeavours. She takes it in her mouth, and for a second it seems he must yield to her completely.

(As I write this now, I realise I'm more likely to raise a laugh than a shiver.)

He pushes her away, she falls, he picks her up brutally, hurls her out the room, then slams the door behind her. He turns to me apologetically. The dawn has finally broken, but so has much else besides.

I push back the covers, get up, it is time for me to leave. But he's already at the door, and when he opens it, in rush two terrifying black dogs.

Think: *Black retrievers*! A thought which frees me, so I catch the more ferocious of the two full in the chops with a kick. Suddenly pacified, the dogs leave the room, whimpering and docile.

I make to leave, and despite knowing I have another session scheduled for the day just dawned, I'm almost sure I shall never see him again – not after what I've witnessed, and the botch he's made of it.

He looks at me sternly, and confidently announces, "So, we'll see each other again in half an hour."

I shake my head. "I don't know about that."

"In half an hour," he repeats, this time imploring me.

I realise now, and this realisation is even stronger than what has just transpired: that he too knows it cannot go on, that it's over.

I know he needs me, but that I must leave him.

I walk out, closing the door behind me. The sun, I note, has only just come up.

It takes me a whole session just to get that dream out. And he doesn't say a word, not even when his wife is giving him the blow-job. I myself have to elaborate, in subsequent sessions, on what is patently some sort of "primal scene", developing all sorts of ideas I probably had as a child about sex and what my parents got up to.

I come back to the dream again and again, with its black retrievers, which he sets upon me, and that agonising look of hope with which he implores me not to abandon him. But there's one thing I never tell him – perhaps there's no need to: this dream is the beginning of goodbye.

At the moment when desire is most intense – his wife's for his penis, mine for his permission to stay, his for my forgiveness for his bungling, mine for his subsequent interpretation, any two parents' for each other, such as will let them conceive a child – is it that then, long before parting or parturition, there's always a *Goodbye*?

I, who had such troubles with "Farewell", was beginning to hope so.

The son has only just been conceived, and already he's out in the sun.

Tuesday 28 November

Forty-nine times out of 50, I ring the door bell after climbing the four flights, and an electronic mechanism operated by the Sergeant from his armchair allows the door to open. (How does he know I'm not a burglar?) But today the door doesn't open automatically. I have to wait. Then the second door opens, on the right of the landing. A middle-aged man scuttles past, to leave the Sergeant standing there. This means there's already someone in the tiny waiting room where normally I'm cloistered. He's going to make me wait in the second, much larger waiting room.

"Bonjour," he says, taking the initiative for once.

"Bonjour."

He gestures to me to take a seat.

"Would you mind waiting?" he tries. "With the strikes, everyone is coming late."

I stare at him incredulously. "What do you mean, everyone?"

He pauses. "Everyone except you."

"Thank you."

Raised eyebrows to ask me again. I shrug. He's off.

Do I mind? After such a concession, I don't suppose I do. Sit comfortably, thawing out. (How to keep the feet warm while on the bicycle? There's a real question.) Take the chance to inspect the Francis Bacon painting.

He comes to fetch me at last. Panic when stretched out on the couch. Hey! I've been dreaming too fast! Too much detail, feel bogged down. Trying to cut to the essential is like staring at one of those magic 3D drawings which are meant to open worlds, but which for me ever remain farcically flat and cluttered. Like trying, and failing, to discern a crossword anagram. Not for the first time, more like the millionth, curse myself for accepting his organisation of the sessions — or disorganisation on a day like today. Means the clock is always ticking, at twice the speed of normal clocks. Then curse myself for cursing, wasting my diminishing minutes in internal digressions.

Start in upon last night's addition to the gallery, just a miniature, which none the less woke me with a start.

"Bearing down upon me is a woman's mouth. I'm backing away from its kiss in terror. But what wakes me, mind, isn't the terror. It's my disgust at my own terrorised reaction."

Before I can even begin to see where this dream might lead me, I'm off again, into the dream of my penis, the bloated cow, the dismembered goat – these have been baying to get out (if cows or goats bay, not to mention penises). Marvel again at the transparency of my member. The Sergeant doesn't seem any more impressed, with a measly "Hmmmm?", than were my fellow sybarites. Squirm again at how my labia have no sensation.

"Do I have to accept, then," I try, "that for my penis to be more than some precious but useless Lalique vase, there'll always be a female tropism attached?"

". . ."

"And that the female will need the male stem if I'm to have any sensation at all?"

(I don't know why I bother going up at the end of my sentences. In 6 years he hasn't answered a single question I've posed him directly.)

The bloating cow seems relatively simple – that "relatively" is important when the stop-watch is running. But the goat? The goat?

See it again, smell it again, and only now recall that running in and out of the urine-stained goat-pieces were children, playing joyfully. A sudden sadness seems to confirm the suspicion that this goat shambles has more than a little to do with my vision, version, of female genitalia.

Member, dismemberment, remembering.

"I don't suppose I have to say it, but I'll say it anyway, though God knows what it means: that these creatures and members are all inside of me, since they're part of my dreams, or more like I'm their dreamer, now their mouthpiece."

"So?" (Ring the bells of Notre Dame! He hath spoken!)

"I'm not just talking about my being hermaphrodite, I've accepted that, whatever <u>accepted</u> means, nor about bisexuality, in the sense of desiring both males and females, even if I'm disappointed that you haven't brought me further out of the closet. What I'm talking about is stranger, and it makes me feel faint."

Pause to breathe deeply, for I really do feel giddy.

"The way in which there's nothing, not a trace of me, not tainted — unless I mean not <u>saved</u> — by being simultaneously its opposite. So I'm drawn and repulsed at once, and there's no resolution. The bloating member is a <u>cow</u>, not a bull, the female shambles is a <u>billy-goat</u>, as if they only existed to be vectors for the switching of longing and revulsion. It's like looking at the famous rabbit's-head–goblet picture, only I'm not just observing some cognitive trick, more like some deviant who can only be turned on by rabbits, or an alcoholic in search of a drink."

Into another litany of complaint about how he has failed to liberate my bisexuality, failed to get me fantasising directly about all-male sex, or better still indulging in it.

"I mean, what on earth am I supposed to <u>do</u> with this great realisation that every damned atom of me contains its opposite? Am I supposed to lie here like some crazed Zen monk staring at his yin and his yang? Where does that get me?"

I don't have an answer. Apparently he doesn't either, since all he does is blow the whistle. "Eh bien." And he stands up to confirm it's over.

Plodding down the steps, I check my watch, and note that today he gave me 25 minutes. Note too, as I curse him for not giving me more after making me wait, that it seemed much longer.

Get on Justine's bicycle and head into the cold, marvelling over my transparent penis. Useless it may be, but beautiful. And the children, playing heedlessly amidst the stench, singing delightedly and delightfully. I hit the absurdly congested traffic on the <u>quai</u>, but that sight and that singing make me smile to myself.

I wouldn't check my watch at the end of every session, though it had been my first instinct for the previous week as I headed down the stairs. What interested me, or what plagued me rather, was the following barely formulated question: In view of the fact that I was soon about to leave, would the Sergeant allot more time to me than usual? Or, as was always possible, *less* time than ever?

After six years of active service, I was surely owed some extra time, a dividend or reward, a token even of some dependence on me which he might have developed ("counter-transference" according to the gloomy psycho-analytic nomenclature). Yet at the same time, he'd better not disturb his routine in the least, lest I start to wonder why he hadn't been allotting me longer all along; lest I start to think of myself as specially deserving (and so specially needy and screwed up); lest – spectre of his imploring face from the dream of "Black Retrievers" – I come to suspect he did in some way depend upon me. And so, getting concentrated into these final weeks, like the pressure in the bicycle pump with which I countered the slow puncture in Justine's tyres each morning, like the pressure which made my dream-cow swell and bloat, was once again the whole problem of time, focused now on how it worked for and against me in analysis, in life.

For despite his name, the Sergeant practised not a regimental session of fifty minutes, but one of variable duration.

"What?" I objected. "Already? You got to be joking!"

I suppose it would have been possible for both of us to do the varying and determine when a session was to end. But in reality I'd cling to the couch, trying in some self-defeating way to "get my money's worth"; which would leave it to him to wave the chequered flag – sometimes just as I was hitting an oil slick.

It's true that when I started I wasn't looking for someone to nurture me or hold my hand. And I'd presumed that the potential explosiveness of the anti-system of the variable-length session would save me from my nightmare of chats and cardigans and tea-cosies, benevolence and sympathetic smiles. I'd read about how Lacan had broken the sacrosanct rule of the fixed-length fifty-minute session, and that it had been one of the principal reasons he'd been expelled from the International Psychoanalytic Association. The unconscious, it was claimed by him and his acolytes, knows no allegiance to chronological time. It issues not like a well-paced argument but in impulsions or pulsations, and so there was no a priori justification for fixing the length of a session. Any such rigidity could only give a deceptive reassurance. Freud, in any case, was never so inflexible in his practice, and the set length of the session was a symptom of the institutionalising priorities of his disciples. If fifty minutes, then why not twenty, one hundred and twenty, or two? Less like a football match, with its set ninety minutes (this was me, not Lacan), than like a Wimbledon final that could go on for hours or be over in a trice. The closing of each session, since it became an event and not just routine, would allow the analyst to say something powerful without using words, intervene directly in the unconscious elaborations, hitting the question back into the patient's court, so making him work towards the next session.

Very well.

But was it not also true that the very variability of the session could rapidly become predictable, especially when constrained by the practical arrangements which have to prevail between any two individuals who intend to meet regularly? Then, if duration was arbitrary, couldn't the argument cut the other way too, and determine fifty minutes precisely because it was so obviously arbitrary? And again, what about the horror stories of seven to ten people all smoking cigarettes in collective waiting rooms of Lacanian analysts, all hoping to be summoned next, only to find themselves out on the street again within five minutes? The logic of *capital* rather than an allegiance to the laws of the unconscious was likely to determine that variability would not mean longer, but almost inevitably shorter – and shorter. And, given the trust which the patient has to put in the analyst to get anywhere, the famous "transference", this meant a virtually boundless scope for abuse – abuse of which I was keen not to become the victim.

Given I'd figured this much out, then why in God's name did I start with someone who told me that he would be varying the length? Was the Sergeant going to extend the sessions to a more reasonable or orthodox length, now he knew them to be numbered? The questions so bothered me as I was cycling round the city that I almost ran down some schoolgirls at Bastille, then almost got myself squashed beneath a bus on the hill of Ménilmontant.

Maybe I'm just a glutton for punishment. Or maybe I found the joke about an analyst being a person who "sells time" too deflatingly consumerist. To the Sergeant's credit, he never cut me off mid-sentence with his usual "Eh bien". Small mercies. He did occasionally bring a rabbit out of the hat (that "Renato", for example), even if more commonly he would wait until I had uttered something which seemed to close one string of associations (or dissolvings) and be about to open another. He had me wait in a room so small it would have given instant heebie-jeebies to anyone suffering from the faintest claustrophobia, and then he'd pull back the curtain just seconds after the previous patient had left (by the second door), with all the bravura of a second-rate impresario. Yet at least that space was for me alone, and even in the larger waiting room I'd never had to share. (My answers to the questions were my usual mix of pros and cons.)

The sessions had quickly settled into an average of twenty to twenty-five minutes, with occasionally one as long as forty or as short as fifteen. But before me, and after me as well, there were others – how could I forget them when only Dan-Daredevil-Cyclist seemed capable of getting there on time? And their sessions had to vary too, yet it all had to work out in the wash, which meant that either I was varying to their rhythm, or they to mine. Unless there was some sort of compromise – but then who ever heard of the *unconscious* making compromises!

The Sergeant is renowned in his field and even to some extent outside it; I'd seen stacks of his books in the Paris bookshops, and it may be that this public endorsement gave me some reassurance. But being renowned, he was also in demand, which meant that the phone would often ring, reducing my already reduced session further, since he would usually answer it, to my unflagging consternation, even if just to tell the caller that he or she would have to ring back.

"'Dans dix minutes," he'd say, "Oui, rappelez dans dix minutes."

Ten minutes? Did he say ring back in ten minutes? So that's how long he's giving me and my measly unconscious!

Maybe I was lucky to get to see him at all, since some were being turned away. But at the end of one particularly truncated session, during which the doorbell rang twice and the phone three times, I asked him if he hadn't thought of setting up shop in an Italian railway station – "Milan, why not, at midday, then you can meet Roberta, since you seem so interested in her breasts. It'd surely be a more peaceful setting than what you're offering me here!"

It's true, I was never bored, never felt I was just going through the motions. But wasn't it a bit like the slow puncture which seemed to be affecting the tyres of Justine's bicycle? Wasn't I simply being conned? Conned by psychoanalysis, especially by this particular formless form of it?

Pros and cons: *pro*fessionals, even *pro*stitutes; and *con*-men, when *cons*, in French, are also *cunts*, and, by a curious deviation, are *blockheads* too, or *idiots*.

Would I be given some grace? Or would the Sergeant stick to his Gunns? I couldn't even formulate the question, with its pros and its cons, without to some extent *giving myself away*. Which giving I desperately wished for – away, away, until nothing remains of me but an essence, the last few cells or grams or gametes that make this human human.

Wednesday 29 November

Talk on the radio of the Government commandeering buses and running them for free to help the strike-locked Paris public. As if that'll help, when it takes a car 3 hours to travel a mile because of the traffic jams. Hitch-hikers abound, none the less. They hardly put out a thumb before a car stops and in they climb, keeping warm at least. The city, transformed from its ferociously individualistic metropolitan self, becomes a cluster of villages linked by routes that are jammed yet strangely relaxed. Cyclists chat to me at traffic lights. And last night, pedalling late to Justine's, a motorcyclist slows down and offers me his arm, to drag me faster to my destination.

Ah, which union boss, high up in the heavens of the CGT or Force Ouvrière, has blessed me with this unprecedented combi of urban paralysis and suppleness? Corresponds so closely to how I feel about myself.

Telephone the lawyer to ask what's happening to my ruined flat. The receptionist answers with, "Oui, Madame. Je vous la passe, Madame." Don't even bother correcting her, I'm so used to it by now: nine times out of ten in French, though never, curiously, in English. Would it be overinterpreting to search here for a reason for my self-imposed exile?

Temperature's dropped another few degrees, but have to leave the Sergeant's waiting-room door open for a minute to let out the heat and the cigarette smoke of the neurotic woman before me (two lipstick-stained butts in the ashtray). Then nip into the bathroom and remove my T-shirt, soaked with sweat from dodging cars and pedestrians.

The Sergeant stares at me when he pulls back the curtain, as if I've just come in from outer space, which the 20th arrondissement probably is to one who works (and, I suspect, lives) plumb in the centre of the city on the Ile de la Cîté. My track-suit bottoms rolled up, my panniers hanging off me, my T-shirt on top – stuff the pretence of Parisian chic, though note that he's as smart as ever.

Scan his room, file for later.

Then, on the couch – hadn't known I'd want to talk about that. The fact that I still don't have a clue, despite my conviction that there must be a central panel, what's to be the subject, plot, storyline or even just the point of departure, for the third part of my Ovine Triptych (third part which is also second or first, given that you can read a triptych in all sorts of ways). Rehearse Parts I and II, as if he wasn't already sick of hearing about them. Almost You, the first book, in which a failed translator wool-gathers shamelessly. One Day as a Sheep, in which it's an old man wool-gathering, on his back, with thoughts racing round his head to which he gives vent, hoping to elicit a reaction from his neighbour and rival, who sits on a bed beside him.

"I can't believe I'm going to leave here without an idea for Part III, when I've been groping around for it for over a year. Not a pinhead of a notion what it could be about. Just that sense of setting out."

"Hmmmm." (An impatient "Hmmmm".)

"Now it's gone, and I'm being aggressed again by a woman's mouth, and aggressed as in my dream by my own feeling of being aggressed."

"Are you afraid it will bite you?"

(Hallelujah! A question!)

"Wish it were as simple as a vagina dentata. I'm not afraid I'll lose a bit of myself, if I kiss a mouth like that I'll lose all of myself, and never get it back. A thousand times more worrisome than coitus. That woman's mouth, I'm afraid it'll become mine."

"It will replace your sex?"

"If my mouth is my sex, then I suppose so."

(My, but he's being voluble today. If he'd been like this some years back, I'd be leagues ahead by now.)

Then on and on about my mouth's defences, the thin Scottish lips, the thick moustache, the perpetually hoarse voice. On and on, until the question: And what if I were just to let myself go, let my lips move forward? Ignore my fear of their own omnivorousness, which is probably what's paralysing me?

But then stop, another image intervenes.

"It's the look," I tell him, "which I saw recently on a suckling mother's face. Inexpressibly erotic, inexpressible for me at least, because inimitable by me or any man."

Wohh! My heart flutters and my breath quickens. All at once I grasp what is for me the absolute erotic appeal of a woman, and why I'll never forgo it.

"Turns," I say, "the way a woman turns. One moment she's making a phone call, cooking the dinner, the next she's giving herself up to be devoured by her infant. Completely passive and completely dominant. And the look on her face, as if in and through that passivity there passed the whole wide world."

Don't need to remind the Sergeant about Eve taking her pleasure, I've told him about it often enough. And what pleasure, on top of, astride me, the most active, violent, and intense pleasure ever witnessed. In moments of interlude I thank my stars I'm regular at my dance class, otherwise I doubt I could take the pace. Inexhaustible, she-dancer, so it's never tiredness or satiety that makes her stop. When she narrows her big owl eyes, glares at me, but I know it's not quite me, nor any other proper name or person, and then – turns.

So grateful to her for that. Oh, I don't just mean turns physically, though that too, onto her front, with her hips raised inches from the floor, allowing me to enter her with more of myself than I knew existed. But psychically, lovingly, though with a love which has little to do with our meagre identities.

All at once an object.

"Use me," she commands. "Use me!"

Hers is the kingdom, and she's so sure of it that she can let me sit in the throne. And I know that, however hard I try, I'll never be able to do what the quaint Scottish vernacular has for fucking, shall never be able to damage her.

I see now, also, that such a turn, even for the most effeminate of men, who can never, alas, give suck, is destined to be impossible.

Lady Macbeth: "I have given suck".

But has she? It scarcely matters. She tells her husband she'd pull her infant from her nipple and dash it on the ground if she'd promised as firmly as she claims he has, to kill the king. If she's willing to give up being queen, she may be saying — then surely she deserves to be queen.

Lady Macbeth: no wonder I've always fancied her most of all Shakespeare's women.

My mouth at last relaxes. "It's not a woman's mouth I see," I tell him, "but a breast, some woman's, impersonal."

I'm the one devouring, and I'm also being devoured — where are the words for that? And for a moment it's as if my whole body will disappear off the face of the couch and earth, with this mix of fright and yearning.

Then I'm back again, and asking him: "And if the mouth, then what about the words that should flow through it?"

"Indeed! Eh bien."

When I wrote above about telling my father's mourners, "I'm off!", I said that "the voice and terms" I was employing were "clearly adult".

I may well have been kidding myself, wishful thinking perhaps. For in the mental ledger of successes and failures of analysis — a ledger whose validity was debatable, since the one drawing it up might be the prime instance of success or failure, without being able to recognise this — one of my prime disappointments was that my voice had not changed. It had remained a child's or adolescent's — an androgen's? In any case so hoarse-sounding and thin that most French people would mistake it for a woman's on the telephone.

Eve said she liked its vulnerability: Pavarotti had nothing to fear.

Each year at my compulsory medical check-up, the doctor would listen to me speak, stare at the "points rouges" on the back of my throat, and advise me to "re-educate" my voice. To which I'd silently reply that I was paying seven hundred and fifty francs a week for just that. Yet it was over two years since I'd spent a day in bed with a cold or sore throat, and as I realised this I only lightly touched wood, whereas in the past I'd have rubbed my naked body across a parquet floor.

My throat, my voice: they were among the very first things I spoke about, the initial time I met the man who was about to become my analyst. Some time when in my building site, between the innumerable unproductive calls to the insurance men and the so-called "Expert" from the Tribunal, I checked to see what I'd recorded about the throat in the journal I kept during those early months.

Here's what I read, first entry in what I should probably entitle, *Danny Ill: Memoirs of a Man of Displeasure*.

Monday 11 February 1990

Morning: tonsillitis tightens its month-long grip, nearly impossible to swallow, but get down the antibiotics (second round; all the first round managed was to make me fall asleep). Voice virtually vanished.

Afternoon: métro to Cîté, and walk to place Dauphine, trying to think what to say. Gloom and doom.

Shake hands, that much reality/banality, but can hardly get my eyes up from floor level. Tonsils ease for the duration of the interview (then take revenge later).

No idea why writing this, but probably a bad one anyway. Decision: not to record here on paper a single word uttered in the sessions. Anything else permissible.

So, enough to say: we talked, and he seemed, if I understood him correctly, to have space for me, or rather time (he seems to practise the variable-length session, so time will indeed be a question).

Enough for one day. Back to bed.

I didn't record the dialogue that was still perplexing me six years on, perplexing me not only because, since analysis reverses the rhythm of friendship, which moves from hesitant beginnings to full conversation, this was more of a *dialogue* than we ever had subsequently.

"My voice," I say to him.

"Is it always like that?"

"I've got tonsillitis or laryngitis, I've got every kind of 'itis' that can live in a throat. But yes, it's always like that, give or take a few decibels. No force in it, so damned feeble, like a child's."

"Have you ever had the experience," he asks me without a pause, "of speaking while you are wearing headphones?"

It takes me a few seconds to grasp the surprising question. "I suppose so."

"And you found the people round you were putting their fingers in their ears, complaining?"

I nod.

"Yet you didn't feel you were straining. So it may not be a physical thing."

"True," I admit.

"So?"

No response to that, unless an obvious one about Peter Pan.

And six years on, still with no response, I felt like asking the Sergeant if he thought I should walk around with ear-plugs permanently in place, that's if I couldn't find a friendly mechanic to turn down the volume control in my brain.

I didn't record that important dialogue, but at least that stricture I put on my journal at the start of my analysis yielded one gain, that my observations on this "frame" were very detailed.

And here I was again taking mental photographs of the Sergeant and his room on those freezing November days six years on. I had inevitably changed over the years, and I knew I was ill-placed to judge how. But he and his surroundings, what the literature calls "the psychoanalytic frame", these had greater objectivity. Could they thereby offer a yardstick for myself?

The two entries after that first interview went as follows:

56

Wednesday 13 February 1990

Sit in a Louis-something chair, fantastically uncomfortable, listening to the noise of the traffic from across the Seine.

Tonsils again.

Concentrate on his English, testing him on his vocab, hope not too obvious. Bit disappointed with results, and disappointed with my disappointment.

Prices are discussed. He says 300 francs a session, and I explain I can't possibly afford that, that 250 is all I can manage, at twice a week. He accepts this. Tuesday and Friday are set as the days.

The couch is alongside the wall, with a bolster for the head, both covered in a sort of oriental carpet. So how has the green velvet of the wall got worn away, almost in the shape of a face or head, right next to this bolster? What horrible convulsions would his patients have to perform to rub away that velvet?

Tuesday 19 February 1990

Rhythm established: métro to Cîté, walk to place Dauphine, up the four flights of stairs, ring the doorbell with the brass nameplate above it: "Dr Renato Sergeant".

Door is opened by some electronic mechanism he activates. Sit on the medieval-looking chair in the cubicle-cum-entrance-cum-waiting-room, curtains on three sides, a mirror on the fourth. (Claustrophobics Keep Out!) Velvet velvet everywhere, and not a drop to drink.

On the wall to the right, candlestick-style electric light, small radiator. Beside the mirror two neat piles of magazines and newspapers, no books.

Hear him pacing past, accompanied, and a second front door closing. So there's a door for going in, another for exiting?

Velvet of his suit too when he pulls back the curtain, quite the magician. Heavy antique table in the corner of the consulting room, stacked high with books and papers, and next to his armchair more stacks, rather messy in fact, an ashtray, letters opened and unopened.

After some minutes, he gestures towards the couch.

What? Already? Well, at least it will get me off this damned chair, maybe that's the idea of having it so uncomfortable.

Hah! There's one mystery solved at least! For almost instantly my right hand rises to my overheated brow, the elbow protrudes to the right, and so rubs against the wall – hence the bald patch. So many brows rubbed in perplexity. Make a point of squashing another few tufts of the velvet to add my trace to those of my predecessors.

At the end, thinking I've figured out the hallway, I lead the way out, through a first door, across a short hallway, through another door, turn right through what appears to be a second waiting room, and finally out through what is indeed a second front door. Must remember to check: was that really a Francis Bacon painting I saw out of the corner of my eye?

Six years on, the bald patch was still there, somewhat larger. He had not redecorated. This was not the Sergeant's home, I'd deduced it from the fact that I turned up early one morning – I forget why the time had been changed that day to eight-thirty – and got there before him. Though the whole floor was his, there was space only for the rooms I'd seen, in addition to the kitchen beyond the second waiting room, from which I'd occasionally hear a kettle whistling. Next to his own consulting room was his wife's, which I was once shown into when I asked him if I could make a phone call. The Bacon painting was still there too, and it was a Bacon. There was a Bram van Velde watercolour hanging on the wall opposite the couch, for which I developed a special affection, probably because of the artist's long friendship with Samuel Beckett.

All these elements of the "frame" were constant enough. But others shifted perilously, whether in my perception of them or in reality (when the line between these two was exactly what I was trying to draw).

"Bring back the Balthus!" I shouted, all the more loudly now that I realised I'd never see it again.

For the first two years it was so prettily above the couch, about a metre from the bald patch, a glorious bouquet of flowers in a youngster's arms, filling my mind with memories of the paintings I'd seen in a Balthus retrospective at the Pompidou Centre: visions of dwarves pulling back curtains, women standing in the most peculiar attitudes, and young girls exposing their pre-pubescent pudenda without the slightest *pudeur*. It hung there provocatively until one day it disappeared, replaced by a painting by Adami, whose work I'd once browsed through and judged to be little more than trendy cartoons in a predictably postmodern mode.

"Bring back the Balthus!" I demanded, even though my very demand was probably making it harder for him to return it to what I deemed its rightful place.

I didn't think much of the drawing which, around the time I announced my sabbatical, replaced the Adami. It depicted some spectral form which if one stared at it – as I did – revealed a face, maybe that of Jacques Lacan. (I never mentioned this to the Sergeant, because either it was my lack of imagination which found Lacan there, or his lack if the resemblance to Lacan was for real.) It wasn't great, but I was glad, none the less, to see the end of the pretentious piece of junk which had ousted *my* Balthus.

"Glad to see," I couldn't resist mentioning, with a snicker, "that you've finally followed my advice in chucking the Adami."

"Hmmmm." (A very sceptical "Hmmmm".)

I watched his personal space closely, observed the mess accrue around his armchair, until one day it would all be clear again and orderly, until a month later mess. The magazines changed, books on his table came and went, the bald patch on the wall slowly grew. I was looking for a sign, to take for a wonder, and failing that as a measure of change.

But I never found either serious transformation, which might have disturbed or inspired me, nor complete fixity either, which, like meeting Rumpelstiltskin or Miss Haversham, might have encouraged me to wake up and change.

And where his "frame" offered no yardstick, his person was even less forthcoming. Gone were the wide-lapelled velveteen suits he'd worn on those first sessions. Now it was some sharp, double-breasted pinstripe from Cerutti or Kenzo. His smoker's cough was worse, to which I alerted him, lingering on the details of the funeral I'd attended in January of a colleague and friend, Jean-François, who had died of lung cancer. Yet if all of this was recognisable, the more important matters were not.

"What's he look like?" Eve would pester me.

I would give a long and detailed description.

"But last time you made him out to be ugly as sin, with short hair and a huge nose. You made him sound like Pinocchio on a bad day."

"No!"

"And now he sounds more like Hiawatha."

I'd be out the room before she'd shout at me, "And his age? What about his age?"

Of course, I'd like to have made an accurate assessment, adding that he'd grown older, by six years, since I met him.

Only, I couldn't. He hadn't!

In these last weeks I was like an archaeologist who must shortly leave a site, determined finally to get the dating right. When I started analysis, I figured he was about sixty six or sixty seven years old. Now, six years on, I made him out to be sixty one or sixty two. By a simple calculation, I figured that he'd grown younger by just the amount I'd grown older. How had he managed this Shangri-La trick?

Certainly it wasn't the black Lotus which I once saw him drive up in. "At your age?" I told him. "Don't you think, since you can presumably afford it" – tone of the exploited – "you'd be better off with a Jaguar or somesuch, most undignified to be driving a sports car."

Though I admit to having been impressed, not to say nonplussed, not to say downright pissed off by the stunt he pulled midway through my time, when he, or more accurately his wife, whom I first saw enlarged, then pushing a huge deluxe perambulator, brought a baby out of the hat reserved for rabbits.

"Really!" I spluttered. "At your age?"

But even as I said it, I could feel his age, and mine too thereby, like two men on their feet in a punt, wobbling precariously.

Thursday 30 November

Yesterday I looked out of Justine's seventh-floor window onto the rue Pelleport below, and there was a solid line of traffic trying unsuccessfully to go up it, only a few cars coming down. Am I hallucinating? Today at the same hour the solid line is heading down it, with only the odd car going up. Strange times, Archie, strange times. And here's me hoping to comprehend something of the esoteric motions of the human psyche!

Pushing Justine's bicycle, one hour later, past a church near the university, when a woman jumps out of the bushes, literally. She's demanding I get a "number" for my bicycle if I wish to take this shortcut. Not satisfied with my response about the exceptional circumstances of the strikes, she shouts at me, going red in the face, accusing me of fouling the path, bringing ill repute to her church — her husband, she informs me, is the pastor — and demanding to know what would happen were there to be a fire.

"What indeed!" I rejoin.

She's shouting again, invoking God's wrath upon me, the students, the striking railway workers, the blacks, and the heathens.

"And your husband?" I turn and ask her.

"What about my husband?"

"He seemed to be enjoying the chaos well enough when I was screwing him behind the altar half an hour ago. I've got a thing for pastors, the proximity to sheep, you know!"

". . ."

Get out while the going's good, thinking: And that too is a woman, that hysteria, bigotry, poison.

In my pigeon-hole, Lacan for Beginners, sent for some unknown reason by the publishers. Think to myself how that's about my level.

After classes, 2¼ hours to walk across the city with my colleague Christopher, pushing the bicycle, "chumming" him as we used to say. Right through the enormous demonstrations on boulevard St-Germain, through the lines of CRS with their batons and tear gas, gossiping as we go.

Now late, and the legs tired from hours on the asphalt. But here are some random pros and cons on the Sergeant that occurred to me today:

Pros:
Ile de la Cîté
Berthillon sorbets, best in Paris, not too far away
his paintings
his lack of interest in holidays
his not insisting I pay when I go on holiday
good magazines in the waiting room (including the ludicrously over-priced art mag FMR)
sense of humour
observant (spotted that cinema ticket I dropped when paying him last week)
pretty wife
child (?)
hasn't changed the price in 6 years
books and journals he churns out (he has other interests)

Cons:
his cigarettes
his telephone

- his lack of interest in holidays (means I never get away without an undertow of guilt)
- his unpunctuality
- the way he shuffles and scuffles behind me (making me think he's disappeared through a trap-door and replaced himself with a gerbil)
- his child's occasional vociferousness, even penetrates all the drapes
- silly sports car
- books and journals he churns out (much more interested in them than in listening to me — in fact that's probably what he's writing when he should be busy curing me)

Off, light, and rub the lamp to let the genie-dream out.

Maybe it's the Woody Allen films that did it, or the stories I'd heard of patients calling their analysts up in the night, or searching through their rubbish bins for an index to their existence, or the books I'd read in which patients keep photos of their analysts in their wallet and turn to them when the going gets rough, or again the one or two patients I've known personally who started to change in appearance or mannerisms, a change I immediately understood when by chance I saw their analysts at some conference, since it was a plain case of impersonation. It's what they call the "transference", which tells that no analysis, therapy, or even medical treatment can be complete without a dose.

It may just be my stubborn nature, which from the moment it sees a well-trodden path will strike out in some other direction, even if straight into a bramble bush. But I just could not get interested. If I'd wanted to find out the Sergeant's true age, for example, it would not have been difficult. But I did nothing of the sort, not even in the final weeks. Nor did I go and buy his books, for the day when I'd be able to read them without their "interfering with my analysis" (as I put it to myself). Did I limit him to the space of the analysis because I feared lest any contact with his real-world persona might actually defuse, not intensify, the transference? Given I had so much trouble investing him with any power or authority, let alone the almost magical capacities necessary to help me move on, maybe avoidance of his mundane self was advisable?

Of course, I'd deduced a fair amount from the "frame", and from circumstantial evidence too. He was successful and unreasonably wealthy, which reassured me somewhat, because it meant he didn't *need* me – those stories flying round of analysts calling up their patients and begging them to come back. That he had a taste in art I appreciated, so I could fantasise I was investing in something I cared about.

All that, yes, but it didn't amount to much compared with what I'd failed to ascertain, had resisted learning, or had more actively disregarded. Oh, the lengths to which I went, they were only now becoming clear to me, as I realised to what a stutteringly inarticulate pass I'd been led, and that there would be no going back and picking up where I'd left off six years before.

I'd made a point of avoiding anyone who knew the Sergeant. I'd avoided asking Christopher about that acquaintance of his who was also seeing him. I even saw less of the friend, Guy Breton, who had recommended the Sergeant to me in the first place. I'd notice where my analyst was lecturing, such as at the École des Hautes Études, and I'd make a point of not attending. I never did more than stare at the front cover of his books in the shops. The only practical information I ever asked him for was telephone numbers of colleagues in the analytic or medical professions who might be able to help friends who were in need – numbers he gave willingly. Not once did I ask the least worldly assistance or advice, though I knew he could have been helpful.

But all that was just the start, the part that was, so to speak, remediable. I went further, much further. For it wasn't just the Sergeant's books on psychoanalysis I neglected to read, but everyone else's as well. And not just on psychoanalysis.

Books of most descriptions, as I've said, became hard for me. I'd manage the first chapter of some text on the theory or history of literature before I realised my eyes were just passing over the words. I flung my book aside so often, and received Eve's advice about practising my dance steps instead, that I even started to make some progress in my *pliés*.

But if I was running out of intellectual fuel, already on reserve tank, then I told myself it was high time I relied on my native wit. Only, that too I was failing to water, when I was not, in wilder moments, laying into it with an axe, lopping off whole branches of my already limited intelligence with what, had it not been for the Canadian association, I'd describe as the nonchalance of an inebriated lumberjack. I reassured myself with whimpers that when analysis was over, I'd go round and recover the branches. But now I knew that they had been floated down the river and turned into pulp. I'd definitely become more stupid, and as I now saw *definitively*, so that sustaining a watertight argument was quite beyond me.

Could such losses be compensated by some gains? In spontaneity, intuition, mental suppleness, or, failing these, in desirability, wealth, perversity – anything? But – and for some reason this lack of a scientific "control" occurred to me as I risked my life cycling round the place de la Concorde – with what would I be able to measure such gains, if not with an intelligence which, so reduced, would be happy to take a bonsai for a sequoia, a flirtatious smile for the notches on the bedpost of an accomplished Don Giovanni. Whereas the stupidity, now that was quotidian, palpable, like a jaw dropping, and with a good line of spittle dribbling from it. Ideas just would not go into this blockhead's brain, into the mind of this *con*, whereas mosquitoes buzzed in and out of the mouth without my even having the canine instinct to snap shut on them.

When, before turning out the light that night, I flicked through *Lacan for Beginners*, I read as much about psychoanalysis as I had in six years. All the old theories, about the "Symbolic, Imaginary and Real", about "The Mirror Stage",

"Foreclosure", about the wonderfully awkward term "Sexuation", about masculine and feminine "jouissance" and the "Graph of Desire" – they all came back to me; but in the way the members of a football team might visit an old and once faithful supporter, who's now been lodged in an asylum. I nodded to them as they filed past my bed, and they told me how they hoped to see me back on the terraces again, waving my rattle and sporting my "Mirror Stage" rosette. I promised them it would not be long before I was back. Yet I breathed a sigh of relief when they left, and went back to the pornographic comic I'd stashed under my pillow when they'd knocked on the door.

Friday 1 December
Morning

And today both directions of rue Pelleport, up and down, are completely blocked.

The dark outside means I get a close look in the window reflection at the scar on my right cheek. Across the street, beyond the traffic, the Hôpital Tenon, where they sewed me up. The one and only time when I managed to shake the Sergeant's usual imperturbability when he pulled back the curtain, covered in bandages as I was, and a good deal of matted blood. He just stood there and stared. Not taciturn for once or waiting for me to fill in his gaps. Simply, literally, speechless.

Hah! I surprised him!

Though he didn't give me any more than the usual 25 minutes – the bastard. Virtually the only occasion as dramatic, in a different way, as the ending that's upon me.

Would like to recall if he asked me, "What happened?" Told him anyway. All I remember him expressing is doubt when I suggest I did nothing to provoke the attack. He is, I can feel it, in so far as I can feel anything beyond my bandages, stitches, bruises, and rage, which have me rehearsing every sort of Scottish football supporter's revenge ever imagined, a string of insults in Edinburgh vernacular not one of which he'd have understood and which would make Irvine Welsh sound like Muriel Spark – he is, I say, as much as I am, confronting a limit to analysis.

Oh aye, I provoked it, if it's provocation to intervene when you come across two women, Eve and Justine, who have just been brutalised by four yobbos, and take the sole remaining one and lay him down gently on his back because you still haven't understood precisely what has happened, when you should have broken his leg or jaw, which would not have been difficult, then hesitate too long, trying to comprehend, until the yobbos return with reinforcements, and from behind you the one who feels humiliated to be have been manhandled swings a bottle he's picked up along the way and breaks it over your face before he and the rest of them run.

Yes, interpret that, if you will.

He does me the courtesy of not trying.

The only time to date, at the end of the session, that I felt like embracing him. Not for his singularly unhelpful doubts. Not for gratitude at anything he did. For gratitude at what, without the slightest endeavour on his part, he simply is: a man. As he probably realised, any man would have done – though no woman, that was certain. (Eve had held and coddled me. It hadn't helped one bit.)

A man, any man.

Did he think he was aiding me by trying to act as if everything were normal? He didn't manage it in any case. Maybe he was embarrassed to have such a bloody mess in his bureau? Oh, he was perturbed all right. Either he really thought I was "acting out" – if only I had been, then I'd have broken the yobbo's neck. Or he thought, precisely, I was not "acting out", thus obliging him to face the limits of his practice.

Questions of limits. My question, now.

(And when I leave his office that day, I go and sit on the banks of the Seine to cry tears of shame and fury. The surgeon who stitched me up has told me she'll make a "belle cicatrice". But the idea of having a "beautiful scar" is scant reassurance. I feel like Frankenstein's monster. Out of the one eye I can still open I see a figure walking a dog along the quai. If it's a man, I tell myself, then I'll go and put my arms round him. He'll hold me. The figure comes closer. It's a woman. Been waiting for that embrace ever since.)

Afternoon

On the couch, recount the genie-fragment from last night: Wandering through the flat of some lawyer, some maître. I reach the end – the end – and open a window onto a garden. But close it immediately since a creature is aiming for me. Leave through the front door, pursued by a bird.

"What sort of bird?" he asks me.

Can't be bothered explaining the slang use of "bird" for a woman. There's another name pressing to get out.

"Right! Un hibou – an owl. Which turns into an obus – an artillery shell. Sergeants. Gunns. I run, but it tracks me, dive-bombs, misses only just, and implants itself on a luxury car next to me – could be a Lotus or a Jaguar, take your pick. It's only then that I see its beauty, like a foot stood on pointe."

I think I catch the drift. Desire to inhabit the Law, stay inside it, inside analysis too, but curious what's outside. Have to escape, but pursued by a woman, an owl could be Eve with her big eyes. But it's only when it/she has missed me that I can appreciate its/her beauty (that balletic foot is surely Eve's).

"Feel it or see it," I say, "never both." And then I'm off again, way back 25 years, walking through Inverleith Park on a frosty Edinburgh afternoon, in the company of Douglas, my classmate. I'm testing him on his French vocab.

"A coffin?" I ask.

"Cerceuil, masculine."

"An owl?"

"Hibou, silent H, masculine."

68

We start to chuckle. Then we have to stop walking because we're laughing so hard. No longer recall if it's for the sound of those two words, or their juxtaposition, or the fact that we've just learned them in class. Maybe just the ridiculousness of language, which means that these sounds signify these objects. We're feeling, 14-year-olds, powers that lift us up from Inverleith Park and drop us down in some immeasurably stranger, more exotic place.

And 25 years on, if I'm soon to be off to Italy on sabbatical, it's partly because Douglas now lives there. Neither of us has quite recovered from the charm of Hibou and Cerceuil.

Stop, think, and can't catch in what language I've just recounted this memory to the Sergeant. The French words in French, presumably, but the rest? In that hybrid of the two languages which has become my staple here?

Ask him, but he refuses to respond.

"Speak up, man! Speak up! In whichever language you choose."

". . ."

Some months before the end, I started in on the Sergeant, warning him that even if he wasn't able or willing to give me an overall summing-up of whatever progress (or the contrary) I had made in my six years with him, there was one subject on which I definitely expected some comment. It was an aspect of our one-sided exchange to which I presumed (out loud) he was attentive: my use of, or use by, the two languages, English and French.

I'm aware, I told him, that the early years were mostly in the former, and the later years in the latter, so he could skip that. I was looking for something more detailed and encompassing. Hence my suggestion that if he were taking notes – all that scribbling behind me – he might want to keep them in two notebooks, in parallel text. I alerted him to the fact that since I was busy responding to the inner prompter, I didn't have time to heed what language I was speaking in. That was his job, for which I was paying him handsomely (never overplayed this card, in case he might take it as time to up the rate).

I was waiting for his commentary, waiting waiting, and reminding reminding – and in the meantime cycling cycling, which in one respect didn't help me at all.

For it was not just the fact of the right-hand side of the road; after eleven years in Paris I'd got used to that, even if I'd never cycled there. It was the completely unpredictable way in which drivers would lunge forward when they finally found some space. I couldn't attribute all the weirdness of their driving to the strikes alone. In the most literal and pragmatic of ways, for some three to four hours each day, my life depended on my accurate interpretation of their *foreignness*.

I'm not the only Scotsman to have felt the tug of foreign parts, and there was certainly nothing exceptional in forever missing the home country. But so what if my homesickness wasn't original? It wasn't only cars I had to negotiate on a daily basis, but a language which, though I spoke it fluently when I arrived in 1984, I knew I'd never feel fully at ease in, and a city which, for all its excitements, would never begin to feel like home.

"Go on," I told him, "let me accept my exile, or let me return home."

Since he was far from forthcoming, I inhabited a limbic region in which I chose to integrate, but never fully, to acquire the language, but never to the point where it might rival my English. I inhabited a restless zone, with welcoming arms of bekilted sentimentality waiting to embrace me every time I opened a bottle of Macallan. And although in most fields I imagined our experiences of life to be so divergent as to give the Sergeant no innate understanding, I genuinely thought that, himself an expatriate, he might have some insights into this domain which he could share with me.

Maybe it wasn't in the "insight" that I was mistaken so much as in the idea of "sharing". For he never called me up to the umpire's box for a word in my ear, only ever returned the ball to me from the other side of the net, in whichever language I served it to him in the first place.

Unless – could it be I really had intimidated him?

I'd noted in my journal, back in February 1990, that I was disappointed with his English. Despite my coyness in writing it down, I shall never forget why. For it may be that my reaction to him then explains why this was one of the last "unforced questions" he posed, or "unforced errors" (as tennis commentators call them) he committed.

We've barely got going on what is only our second session, when – "Did you make any dreams," he asks me, "since the last session?"

"*Have*," I correct him automatically. "Did I *have* any dreams?"

I bite my tongue, too late. He tries not to wince, and I try not to either. The silence which ensues is a torture. He doesn't stand a chance, and I don't either, with the way I've been schooled, through tweak of ear and lash of taws on outstretched palm. That *make any dreams* is a straight translation of *faire des rêves*; but it's almost enough to stop me in my tracks and make me try someone else.

Did he feel inhibited from the outset by my scolding? I tried to compensate by pointing to my weaknesses: the genders which were almost completely interchangeable, the confusion I made between hard and soft *us*, the dyslexic gnome living inside of me, who lets me pick up a foreign accent at the drop of a hat, but then makes me forget how to spell even the most basic of words.

Yet he would not bite.

Did I *make* any dreams? It was perfectly logical, what is more. I wish, for his sake and mine, that I could have brought sense and usage into line. But in the end we only spoke a language of hybrids and mongrels, *between* two grammars and lexicons, where we both had to venture, and were forever being caught out. We did not, then, have a language.

We *made* one.

Saturday 2 December

From the lawyer's message on the answering-machine, deduce that there's no chance I'll get back into my flat before I leave for Scotland on Christmas Eve – with Eve? By which time analysis will be over.

Every day, then – Thank you, Justine – I'll be staring across at the Hôpital Tenon, feeling my scar, thinking also of the 3 HIV tests I've had done there. Each time to be told by the doctor that while it was good to be sure, I shouldn't feel over-anxious, given all the precautions I was taking.

(Very attractive too, the last doctor, a woman in her forties. After she hands me back my life on the slip of paper which says "Séronégatif", she asks me if I have any questions. What sort of questions? Many people, she explains, worry about different types of sex, and the risks involved. Oh, absolutely. She goes through the various perils of saliva, blood, and semen, on which I'm already expert. Me thinking I shouldn't be so excited.

"Et le contact bucco-anal, par exemple?"

Wow! She's stumped me there, I'm agog. "Par exemple," I get out, wondering what the French is for "rimming".

"Il semblerait que cela ne pose pas trop de risques."

I nod sagely, as if she's just told me that the vicarage lawn needs watering.

Beautiful. And I ask myself why I live in France!)

Then, beyond the hospital, so I can see the tops of its trees, the Cimetière Père-Lachaise, where I like to wander. Where, on a marrow-freezing day in January we paid our last to Jean-François. He so young, brilliant, generous, helped me through my early years in Paris. Everywhere I turn there's a death. This can only become more the case, the older I get.

Even with Eve, when we meet for lunch today. She's looking great in her short red skirt.

"So you're really going to abandon me for Italy?" she says.

I'm trying to figure out if she's being serious or has the tip of her tongue in her cheek. Get distracted when I spot a corpse on the horizon.

"Not abandon you, come on. You know you're welcome to visit. I'm only going for nine months."

"The way you betrayed me with Roberta."

"My, but we are being classical today!"

"It's not just your body I'm talking about, it's your mind in flight."

A wave of sadness breaks over me. "We're all going to die," I say, and it comes out melodramatic.

"What," she says, picking up my portentous ball and running with it, "even your wise old marabout?"

"He's a doctor, should know better, Gitanes his crutch, nothing 'light' about them. He's ignored all my warnings. Yet barring accidents, it does seem he's going to see me out. You know how much time I've spent warning him he wouldn't make it, that his assumption he'll survive leaves me cold?"

Of course she doesn't know, nor is she interested.

I admire her legs as she jumps to her feet and leaves me to the remains of my pasta.

Wonder now, though, if I haven't got this dying business completely back to front.

I continued to tell the Sergeant that whatever else might have changed in my life since starting analysis, one thing remained constant: that my own life grew out of another's death, my father's, when I was five years old. Despite what he claimed to the contrary, implicitly where not explicitly: that I could be plural and could change.

For six years the Sergeant received me, except during his three weeks of annual holiday, at more or less the same time, give or take a few minutes, two and then three times a week, never once missing a session for ill-health. Of course, he's smart enough to have known that to pretend he was "there for me", "wouldn't abandon me", or any such sweet-sounding empathic nonsense, wouldn't cut any cadavers with one like myself. For I'd had just such a father: there one day, gone the next (and the next and next and next). If he imagined that by his very constancy he could correct in me what mere words and intentions could never manage, then he was in for a letdown. He'd never convince me through sheer experience that there could be other sources in my life than here-today-gone-tomorrow. He'd never relieve me of the nausea I'd felt at going to school each morning, convinced that when I got home I'd find myself an orphan.

For his method was based on a risible premise of predictability. And any day now – even with just a few weeks to go, it was never too late – I'd climb his stair, ring the bell, and be met by his wife, who'd tell me that "le docteur Sergeant" was ill-disposed, in hospital, or already six feet under. I would, quite simply, because I *could*, and he had no way of refuting it.

His mistaken premise was that he could predict the future, and thereby invent new futures for me. A mistake which the fact that it did now seem he'd outlive my presence in his life did nothing fundamental to rectify. A mistake which came from imposing an incremental logic on what was absolute and arbitrary.

"You could be here every single day for sixty years, and it still wouldn't work."

Admittedly, the more I needed him, the less likely he was to be there, which seemed to indicate that even the arbitrary and absolute could become invested with private significance, and so be susceptible to change. But what of it. I was none the less convinced, that is I *felt* convinced (which was surely what mattered) that, as I put it to him: "You're confusing *trust* with *faith*".

To make completely sure he grasped what I was on about, I translated the idea into French. Or rather I tried to translate it, only to find it would not go. *La foi* would more or less do for faith, but what did we have for trust? *La confiance? La fiabilité?* But these terms had no real depth or gravitas, like when speaking of "home" I had to say "chez moi". And, if trust wouldn't work, then faith, with which it contrasted, was surely askew as well.

"Trust," I told him, "you'll just have to hear it in English. And faith."

". . ."

"You know I've got no special problem with trusting the people I like and respect. I count on them for the everyday rewards and satisfactions. I've got friends I'm in close daily contact with, since I was a child, they support and love me, and I love and trust in return. Listen, I don't need you to teach me how to trust, you got that?"

"Ah bon?"

I meant it too, I didn't need to learn to live with that painstaking combination of the possible, the pleasurable, and the perilous that is trust. I needed him to teach me – when *teach* is quite the wrong word – not trust, but faith. Only faith would relieve me of that single story of how the axe was always about to fall, and would open up new and unpredictable futures, bring me fully to life at last.

"Faith *in?*" he asked me.

"That's not the point. Though not in *you*, and certainly not in psychoanalysis, please!"

I didn't have an answer, and so I went on brooding. Faith he could not teach me, because then I'd have to learn it, and I'd be back in the empirical domain of trust. Faith which had been broken, and which would now have to be passed down, conferred from above – it should drop like bird-shit on my head more than like the tablets handed down to Moses.

"Only with such faith," I told him, "will I ever begin to overcome my paternity prohibition, for example, or resolve my relations with my homeland, or end this analysis in other than admission of defeat."

Sergeant Stone-wall. Maybe he was content that my interest in him, bypassing any fascination with his life or work outside of this room, ended by elevating him to the status of demigod.

There's a definition given by Lacan of the "transference", which turns the analyst into a "sujet supposé savoir", a "subject supposed to know" (as it is usually translated). It's the "savoir" bit which is always picked up and commented on by theorists of analysis, but it's the "supposé" which is at least as important, of which "supposed" is but a dim reflection. For I may not have invested the Sergeant with much knowledge of me, surface or depth, but I had certainly put him *up there*. I hadn't so much "supposed" or "presumed", more like I'd "placed him on top" – *sup-posé*. I had "put him up there", imagining not that he knew me, nothing so modest or believable, but that he was the holder of the single great unnameable gift, the one you can never earn, deduce, or conjure for yourself, however hard you try: the gift of faith.

Sunday 3 December

Desire to "be analysed" = desire to see the world more clearly? Yes, divested of the clutter you're continually throwing onto it. The tough thing being, as in last night's socialising at Eve's flat, that you become less and less tolerant of other people's clutter as well as of your own.

Only, that's not right either, since it implies censure. In fact it's just that other folk's confusion of themselves and the world becomes less and less interesting. Such distances! With a few more years' analysis I'd end up being able to converse only with those in analysis, though I'd be too uninterested even to bother doing that. We'd all sit round, as in some gentlemen's club to which analysis alone could ensure election, not bothering to converse, just staring into space, or at blowflies or dust which we'd henceforth be able to see with lizard's-eye precision. Occasionally darting out a tongue, not to catch the fly, but just to let it know that we could have, had we wanted to.

Fortunate call, then, from my editor at the TLS, asking if I'll review two books for a French issue due out in January. I say yes, though when am I going to find time to read them, let alone write about them? Le Testament français by Andreï Makine, and La Langue maternelle by Vassalis Alexakis. Both books by foreigners writing in French, which makes me feel on home ground. Unless the ground is, rather like me, "away from home"?

Evening

Trek to the university to use the computers and mark term papers, thinking: my relation to my students will change when I stop analysis, but how? They surely don't take me for a demi-god, but they do appear to believe I know something they don't. Never imagined a neutral position vis-à-vis students. There's certainly nothing neutral in the way the Sergeant treats me. Spared by Paris and the whole of French culture from the ravages of political correctness which obliges pre-judging the real human stakes and issues. There are no clear areas, least of all in literature, no zones free of the need to seduce and be ravished.

Two of my keener and more interesting students ask me out for a drink. Conversation tends to reveal the gaps more than the connections, but I'm busy in any case thinking about not becoming a lizard.

Stolid lucubration in café, thus: By refusing to give what the other thinks he or she wants, as the Sergeant presumably does to me and as I probably do to my students, is one encouraging this other to think harder about what it really is that he or she wants? I'll magically find I want to be myself. My students will magically find they want to read more books. All fine and dandy. But by seeing a student's being drawn to me in terms of "transference", maybe I'm not avoiding narcissism at all. Maybe the opposite, being as narcissistic as possible, because forgetting that he or she might be drawn to me precisely for what I do not know.

Oof! Down that kir, and order another, a double.

We all botch our deaths, I suppose, since we're never present at them. But psychoanalysts could be defined by the interdiction on botching theirs. And it is this, much more than any esoteric knowledge, that makes them neighbours of magicians, saints, or shamans.

Was this the notion, along with a powerful counter-example, which, compacted by the ending almost upon me, led me to wonder if I hadn't got my view of the Sergeant's endeavours all back to front?

He was convinced that, beyond anything he could say, he could inspire some faith in me, because he was also convinced that he would survive me. Or so I always believed, and against which belief I always militated. Until, in these last weeks, I thought: and what if he were indeed to drop down dead today, with so little of the analysis left?

For, if analysts must not botch their deaths, then I knew one who just had. In April Justine's Sergeant had died.

She'd been seeing him once a week for almost two years, and from what she told me about him, he sounded like a wise therapist and a thoroughly likeable man (I was far from sure I could say the same of *my* Sergeant). Though what Justine told me made the sessions sound more like heartening conversations than strict analysis or therapy, I could see the effects clearly, as old fears and detritus were discarded and a new lightness prevailed (see them so much more clearly in her than in me).

Then, one day in April, she showed up as usual and was not admitted. The following day she received a letter from her analyst's wife explaining that her husband was severely ill. The next letter announced his death.

Between her tears when Justine was telling me all about it, I saw her need to mourn. But, though I didn't tell her, I also saw the silhouette of a figure that looked just like my faceless father: there one day, gone the next. He had just committed the one unpardonable error, which no amount of mourning could ever cover.

What would I do if the Sergeant dropped dead, with just three weeks to go?

The answer, surprisingly, was simple: get back into analysis. For Justine, such a suggestion would probably have sounded like I was proposing she trample upon her analyst's recently dug grave. Me, I wouldn't have hesitated for a second, and as I trampled across the Sergeant's grave I'd wear hobnailed boots heavy enough for him to feel them, six feet under.

"You see," I plagued the Sergeant, "just as I told you. And he wasn't even a smoker. The fact that you think you can teach me by example if not by precept – it won't hold water." I snapped my fingers in the air.

He said nothing.

But though I taunted him with mortality, the certainty I felt about what I'd do, if he died, was shifting me around. Maybe it wasn't the case at all that, convinced of his own immortality, he believed he could inculcate a new faith in me just by being there, and could keep his mouth shut until that happy day. Maybe, on the contrary, he was convinced of his own *mortality*.

Knowing that death is the event which we all, even analysts, are destined to botch, he'd perhaps decided, and this practically from the outset, having measured the effects of the prior death upon me, to ensure, by his regularity, his distance, his self-effacement, his impersonality, that the analytic process would never, ever, become identical with his person. Were he to die, in this way I'd not go down with him – for while one such death may be tolerable, and even have, as I'd recently found, its liberating aspect, two would spell disaster.

I hadn't only found a new answer to the question of what would happen if he dropped down dead today, for the very terms of the question had changed.

"Eve's muscular thighs wrapped round my back, her short red skirt hitched up around her breasts."

"Uhhh?"

"Just checking you're awake. Listen now, get this into your skull, as my teachers used to say to me: Just because there are only three weeks left, you needn't start thinking you can die on me now. Even if it's just for these three weeks, I'll find a replacement for you, believe me, and I'll see it out with him. Yes, that's me. In your own mould. Just that cruel, just that callous."

And I did not say, though I wondered – just that *faithful*?

He didn't die, let me make that clear now. Nor did I.

We outlived each other.

Monday 4 December

Announced on the radio this morning that the Government has commandeered bâteaux-mouches to transport the strike-bound public up and down the Seine. And when you want to get off? They're presumably leasing out life-buoys, so the passengers can jump. They'll be floating Montgolfiers next, distributing parachutes, to get businessmen to their appointments. And it's all grist to my egotistical mill. Including the sense which everyone in Paris seems to be sharing, that the apocalypse is nigh.

Must prepare my final class, try not to go out with a whimper, as Julien Sorel climbs to the guillotine at the end of our final text, Le Rouge et le Noir.

What does Julien die for in the end? Not for killing Mme de Rênal, since he only grazes her with his bullet, she pleads for him, and then she follows him to the grave. Nor even for his hateful intentions, since he knows she's the best person he's ever met, and since the accusatory letter she's sent which prompts him to violence only contains the truth, in any case, about his social climbing. Nor does he die for the cause he tries to espouse in court, of the class war, or of the new Napoleon trying to renovate History. All that's clear is that he's far from clear. And Stendhal none too clear either, or at least his patronising, interfering narrator. What's Julien's crime? As that clever critic Peter Brooks suggests (at this rate I'll be able to read from my journal in class!), maybe Julien's crime is one of trying to usurp his own story, upstage that paternalistic know-all narrator, cease being a passive plaything of the various father-figures who determine and overdetermine his life, at last actively take hold of his destiny – even if he does attempt it in such a ludicrous way. At which point the very incomprehensibility of the crime, and the inappropriateness of the punishment, become in some self-destructive and laughable way emblems of Julien's success.

Strange times, Archie, strange times indeed, when you have to go to such lengths to become the subject of your own story. Raskolnikov's just a few doors down the block. Though at least his crime's got an edge to it.

Subject for the day, as I cycle round the city: crimes one could commit.

After midnight

Didn't get far with the crimes, because all my concentration needed not to get run down. (I don't suppose imitating a flattened pollo alla diavola on the tarmac would admit me deep into Inferno.) I'm taking my life not so much into my own hands as into those of the Parisian drivers, avoiding their doors which flash open and threaten to take your leg off, then dodging crazed motorcyclists who virtually do wheelies down the pavements, novice roller-skaters who spin round the lamp-posts to which they've attached themselves – all to go and speak to a man who remains silent. It's enough, in the circumstances, to prove one must be crazy. And so that I should be getting back on the bike, en route for the next session.

Exhausted, switch on the TV at 11 and am immediately hooked by the start of David Mamet's film House of Games. Talk of cons and conning!

It's beautifully done, and in my present context most disturbing too. Something wrong with the ending, though, when the analyst twigs, cracks the plot against her, tracks down Mantegna with the money, and shoots him dead. It's perfectly consistent in a way, but somehow all wrong. Too late and too tired to try and figure out why.

Everyone has a voice, except the mute or the autistic, and nearly everyone finds that voice hard to hear. Writers, all sorts of writers, of letters, reports, articles, books, writers have an extra sort of "voice", which takes a lot of training to develop but which can also be hard to overhear.

"But I'm not just like everyone else," I tried to convince the Sergeant. "I'm worse!"

"Oh yes?"

In these final weeks my voice didn't drop an octave. I still found it unbearable – not just like everyone else, truly *unbearable* – to hear it on a tape-recorder.

"Who's that pip-squeak?" I asked Christopher after I accompanied him home after our traipse across the city. He'd switched on his answering-machine, and for a good few seconds – which became retroactively an *excruciating* few seconds – I was scoffing at that throttled utterance.

"Oh shit, it's me."

All such indignities might be tolerable, I told the Sergeant, if there were some new gains in that other voice I was trying to find when writing. But here I was, with the clock ticking away, and not a clue what I was going to write next, the central panel of my triptych still a blank. Surely it would be *ovine*. But I'd never find its outlines by concentrating on this fact, since the two other panels had revealed their ovine lineaments only gradually, with the sheep coming of their own volition to the rescue.

Add to my doubts about the future my quibbles about the past. All those pieces I'd written, stories, novels, screenplays, which I'd failed to push or promote. The money I squandered at Papier Plus, the expensive paper shop where I bought the books of unlined A4 paper in which I like to write. The whole drawer of my filing cabinet that's full of unpublished pieces. The *laissez-faire* way I'd let the dust gather, claiming my words could only reach sympathetic ears.

"But that was then," I explained to the Sergeant. "Now it's different. Now I'm determined that from the moment I write my next book, then my bleats will echo round the glen."

Tuesday 5 December

Last night get to sleep late after starting that book for review by Andreï Makine. I hardly seem to have dropped off before I wake – am woken – in the wee hours. Sit bolt upright, staring round in the dark of Justine's bedroom. Someone has spoken my name! Not in my dream, but wrenching me <u>out</u> of the dream in which I was deeply engrossed. "Danny!" the voice says, just once, but urgently, and clear. A man's voice I don't recognise. Switch on the light, sit there trembling until the dawn rises. Doze for half an hour.

In those few minutes of sleep, dream I'm arriving in the Sergeant's office and telling him something, quickly, that's the very dream I am dreaming.

But before I can get started he says to me: "C'est toujours mieux de garder ses grands rêves pour soi."

Waking up is like emerging from some Borges story from which you're never sure you've emerged. Get dressed and onto the bicycle, replaying in my head what he said (in my head): "It's always better to keep one's big dreams to oneself".

The heat in the Sergeant's office after the freezing air outside, added to the lack of sleep, puts me into an instant daze as I stretch out on the couch. Trying to think whose voice called to me during the night, and what it tried to say to me.

"Maybe the voice that hailed me was my father's? I've been wanting to hear it for long enough."

"Hmmmm."

"I want to hear him, just once. The home movies are all silent on which he appears."

". . ."

"But why would he be speaking to me, now of all times? Went to sleep wondering about my writing."

The Sergeant doesn't respond, and suddenly his window rattles violently as if it's about to burst in. Turn on the couch and look out at thick snow gusting past in great big clouds. Cycling in this is going to be no joke, especially as today is the official high-point, the "point noir", of the strikes, which means postal workers are out too, and Telecom, anyone who feels like it, blocking the already blocked traffic. But a child's delight at the sight of the snow, and I'm getting out the sledges, preparing for chilblains. A thousand memories of when winter was really winter, in a Scotland the Sergeant doesn't know.

"In my dream," I try, "you tell me that 'c'est toujours mieux de garder ses grands rêves pour soi'."

"Eh oui!" That's the most enthusiastic response I've heard from him in weeks.

"What do you mean 'Eh oui'? Why 'oui'?"

". . ."

"Oof!"

"Eh bien."

"Wait a second," I insist. "C'est mieux — it's better, because big dreams engender little dreams."

"C'est ça!" he exclaims.

Then he's up on his feet, and I'm out into the white-out.

I tried to imagine: If that voice which called to me during the night, from outside the realm of dream, was my father's, then what was it trying to tell me?

I imagined it was trying to tell me to wake up, precisely, quit dreaming.

What was I dreaming about?

Since I couldn't remember, I had to imagine that too. I was dreaming I *was* my father, or all that was his: the house, the Danish furniture, the Jaguar car, nothing frivolous or flamboyant, but everything beautiful and stylish. I was dreaming of the business he started, going from bricklayer to boss, employing some fifty-odd men to build houses which became *homes*. I was dreaming of his successes, of all that was his when he was cut off – cut off in his prime. I was dreaming I was he, and that his accomplishments (now mine through the dream) would be nefarious, mortal, fatal.

"Wake up!" the voice told me, "you're dreaming. Success need not kill you."

Analysis and crime. Despite the misguided ending, Mamet was surely right: they are ideally suited to one another. The plot of *House of Games* is a gem.

A highly controlled woman psychiatrist, author of a recent bestseller called *Drives: Obsession and Compulsion in Everyday Life*, lacks some excitement in her own career-driven life. She takes the chance to pay off a patient's bad debt, and visits the "House of Games", where she immediately gets adopted by the man (played by Joe Mantegna) to whom the patient is supposed to be in debt. He employs her to watch for the "tell" which will give his opponent's bluff away in a card game. She helps him, but he loses; she's about to pay the now much bigger debt, when she realises she's being conned. And so, she thinks, she becomes one of the club. The intimation being, of course, that as a psychiatrist whose con-trick is the "transference", she is *already* one of the club.

Joe Mantegna explains the philosophy: he, as con-man, pretends to give his victim his confidence (or trust); and in return for that rare human commodity his victim is more than willing to give his confidence (or trust) in return, and to pay for the privilege.

But in fact the psychiatrist is just being set up for a bumper-sized con in which all her hard-earned savings are going to be blown in a single go. All the previous revelations were only screens, and everything she thinks she has penetrated is only illusion, theatre, staged by the con-men. Drawn by her fantasy that she can finally enter real life, she finds herself playing a part whose every line has been rehearsed.

She finally twigs, though, and that's where it all goes wrong, not just for the con-men, but for Mamet as well.

Wednesday 6 December

Cycle furiously from the university to Château d'Eau so as to get to my dance class on time, endangering my own life and that of several pedestrians. Motivated less by the idea of <u>grand</u> <u>plié</u> or <u>développé</u> than of lying flat on my back on the floor. Arrive just in time, get myself and bicycle into the lift (no leaving it outside, bikes are more precious than cars these days). The doors close, the lift rises a few feet, then jams. And will neither up nor down. Try the alarm. It refuses to ring. Thank the deities for all my practice in the Sergeant's cupboard-waiting-room, and start slamming on the door – quite enjoyable in its way.

A man's voice finally shouts to me from a distance, asking if I'm stuck.

"Yes, I'm stuck! Oui! Je suis coincé!" I confirm at the top of my voice, trying not to think of what might be the metaphysical implications of this statement.

"Ne vous affolez pas, ma'moiselle! On vous sortira de là!"

And for 40 minutes this unknown man and some benign colleague endeavour to get me out, shouting all the while to me – "Ma'moiselle!" – not to panic (which I have no intention of doing), while I reply that I'm still alive and am grateful to them for their efforts.

Six years of analysis, and I'm still not even "Madame". Think to advise them, but fear they'll just leave me there if they find that out.

And oh, the look of disappointment on their faces when finally they get me back to the ground floor and crowbar open the doors.

"Mais — mais, c'est un mec!"

"Eh oui, hélas!" I commiserate. 'Tis a man (more or less). And I mean my "alas", for they're rather a toothsome pair. I'd happily let them hug me as recompense for their efforts.

Before that little drama, on the couch, a dream fragment, in which a smartly dressed man whose face I can't see is signing copies of his new book. He's holding a glass of champagne in his hand, and on the wall behind him is a row of cubicles, each of which contains a beautiful half-naked woman, all of whom are at his disposal.

Hardly necessary to say much about such transparency. (Though haven't I seen that word "transparency" recently, attached to my penis?) A phrase comes back to me, which my mother has used of my father: "Champagne tastes on a cider budget". Must have referred to their early days together, since by the end, his end, he was living in some style.

Success = fatality?

Hear the Sergeant scribbling away behind me. Warn him that by writing he's only ensuring that I shall take my revenge. Don't elaborate on this though, since I've no precise idea what it means.

Summings-up have never been my strong suit, which may partly be why I was expecting so much of the Sergeant. When I ask myself what sort of writing, what sort of art, is appropriate to our era, an era which has known so many grand ambitions, projects, theories, totalising concepts and ideologies, and which has suffered at their hands, I tend to turn to one of the most moving, insightful, prophetic, and *short* statements on modern art I know. In it, Samuel Beckett tells art historian Georges Duthuit of the necessity for an artist to experience an "insuperable indigence" before his search for form, and of the artist's duty to fail, "as no other dare fail".

Beckett is surely right. In our era, the "aesthetic of failure" he proposes, even if he has to do it, as in his dialogues with Duthuit, through jokes, self-effacement, paradoxes, is a coherent and humane one.

However, add to this my fears about my father's successes. Add to that a genuine distaste on my part for much of what the world deems success, an allergy to Sunday newspapers and their supplements, a John Knox censoriousness towards anything boastful or brash (that came along with toilet-training). And what do we find? Not just all the ingredients for complete, permanent, and irreversible anonymity. We find a latterday Dr Jekyll.

Of course, even Dr Jekyll could see that Beckett's plays are great successes, maybe the greatest successes of our times. Despite myths to the contrary, Beckett tirelessly promoted his own work, trying to get it into the public eye, *notwithstanding* his deep-felt reservations about it (until he found professionals better equipped than he to do it for him). But measuring anything I might write by Beckett's standards would be like trying to compare my dwarf *développé* to that of Sylvie Guillem.

And wasn't I ambitious too?

Long before I stumbled, unknowing, into my first Beckett play and was hooked for life, I was playing the board-game "Careers" with my mother and brother. I used to divide my winning ambition between thirty points "wealth" and thirty "fame"; while they, who always lost, staked their careers on oodles of "happiness", which was symbolised by a heart.

"That's just like you," Eve said when I told her about it. "Heartless."

And then, more immediate than Beckett's double-edged ambitions and successes, or the recollection of my childhood vainglory, here was this ending coming upon me.

For, however hard I tried to ignore the need for recognition, hoping this would amount to my own "insuperable indigence", and would save me from being the next to be "cut off in my prime", I was never going to manage it – or at least never manage it as well as the Dr Jekyll I had sitting right behind me: Dr Sergeant Jekyll.

For six years he had been as modest as a mouse, as tight-lipped as a Wee Free minister on a dreich Sunday morn. And yet even this was not going to save him. Hyde he would become. Notorious.

If you can't join 'em, beat 'em. Big dreams make little dreams. I was starting to have an inkling what these dreams I shouldn't tell him might consist of.

Thursday 7 December
Afternoon

Give my final class of the semester. Julien Sorel is guillotined at last. Prospect of not having to open my mouth again to lecture for 9 months is like waking up and thinking you're late, then remembering it's the week-end and you can stay in bed till midday. Feel a bit like a soldier just demobbed, smiling at my students like we're all civilians now. I'm no longer the one supposed to know.

Smartly dressed elder statesman on the traffic-blocked quai d'Orsay just along from the Ministère des Affaires Étrangères, looked just out of a Cabinet meeting. Staring at the snow-thick sky as I cycle past, he shouts, at the top of his voice, "J'en ai marre! J'en ai marre!"

Turn your flat into a ruin, Minister, then you too can enjoy the strikes. Start analysis!

Later, in the Go Sports mega-store in Les Halles, trying to buy myself a front light for the bicycle. But they're all sold out. A shoal of about 200 bicycles, 10 shop attendants working furiously on constructing more of them. And a customer is being warned that all of them will be sold by this evening. It is the closest I've come, and even old-timers are saying it, to a city under siege.

Night

How all occasions do inform against me, Horatio.

Eve calls to remind me we're due at the theatre this evening, to see Peter Brook's new production at the Bouffes du Nord, something called Qui va là? It turns out to be a truncated Hamlet (just what I don't need in my present state), with reflections on theatre and acting thrown in from Stanislavsky, Brecht, et al. Always clever enough, Brook, to know not to try being cleverer than Shakespeare (contrast Peter Greenaway's Prospero's Books). Aware that in just one third of the play there's more than enough for an evening, if you can get that third right.

I'm busy watching the crafty way he's reduced the play down to the parts explicitly about performance, admiring the fine acting, translating it back from French into English in my head. All the while thinking: I could have done without the reminder of Hamlet's dad — "Cut off even in the blossom of my sin" — and of all those leave-takings for which the son is so ill-prepared. Act 3 Scene 4, in Gertrude's bed-chamber, unbearable at the best of times, feels tonight like the most borderline thing in Shakespeare. And then that name, Gertrude, how hasn't it occurred to me before, the little-known first name of Sargent's Lady Agnew of Lochnaw, she on whose lap I'd like to sit.

Dinner after, out, a relief and a rare treat, down the road at the Terminus Nord. Eve looking great with her hair up and her eyes flashing. Being nice to me, that feels like a rare treat too. The waiters, for some reason, instead of their usual brasserie black and white, are wearing kilts and sporrans. There's Scottish dishes on the menu too — most confusing.

Hamlet in French, brasserie in Scots. I'll never be po-mo.

Remark to the waiter that his kilt should probably stop <u>above</u> the knee, not two inches <u>below</u> it, but he looks at me as if I don't have a clue. Think of the time in my bank when, after I'd spelled out my name, the clerk stared at me with fine French incredulity and said, with no trace of irony: "Vous êtes sûr?"

First time Eve's invited me back since I was ejected that morning two weeks ago. She doesn't hang around either, and I do my <u>heartless</u> best.

After, sit in her bathroom, jotting these notes. Keep the door locked. This journal, it's not yet a "grand rêve", but it's getting bigger by the moment.

From a guffaw in the office at work, I realised some time around now that I'd started, perhaps under pressure of the forthcoming end, to say, when announcing my name over the phone, "Monsieur – non, pas Madame – Monsieur Goon". I'd still have to spell it out – G-U-N-N – but at least they could repeat the sound back to me, which was impossible when I pronounced myself correctly.

Was this attempt to translate my name just a convenience, given all the lawyers, builders, and insurance men I had to call about my ruined flat, or was it a last-ditch half-hearted attempt to integrate? Here I was, about to leave France for Scotland, thence to Italy, and now, only now, I was pronouncing my name in a way the French could hear it.

Hamlet goes to Wittenburg, but comes back; goes to England, but returns (though his old pals do not). You don't have to hit him with an Oedipal sledgehammer to see he's having a hard job getting out from under his parents' shadow, struggling to say goodbye – despite his histrionics in Ophelia's grave. And this isn't quite the same thing as saying he hasn't learned to mourn, since it's also the living he fails to leave behind.

I'd often said to myself that by the time I had resided away from Scotland for as long as I'd lived there, I'd be able to return for more than a holiday. Then, when that didn't work –

my thirty-fourth birthday came and went, and I was still ensconced in Paris – I told myself it would become possible when analysis ended.

Of course, since all occasions were informing against me (as the man said), the two novels I'd agreed to review were about leaving the home country, Greece in one case, Russia in the other, and the pain and excitement of that wrench. Everywhere I turned I was finding reflections of my doubts and desires – I who'd imagined myself the lizard of objective disinterest.

You enter therapy or analysis – I don't think I'm exceptional in this – expecting to find within yourself something peculiar, singular, intensely personal, probably inadmissible. Even if you don't have the ambition of taming them, you do imagine monsters, grotesques, depths, Acheronta. Yet what the approaching end was telling me was that I was discovering something simple, somewhat impersonal, as if genetic or generic; and it was floundering in the shallows rather than lurking in the depths.

When Justine badgered me about why I persisted in my analysis, my stock response was: "So as to become more superficial". It was fine just saying it, but now the little flounders had their tiny teeth round my toes, and they tickled more than hurt. It hadn't needed six years of thrice-a-week analysis to inform me I had a bit of a Hamlet complex. I wasn't the first Scotsman to enjoy crying into his whisky to thoughts of the '45.

Humbling, humbling.

Only, what mattered was not what I understood or where I was unique. Let me be made like everyone else, I thought – only let me make anew. Let me know as much as I can, but the better not to know.

And if I'm to paddle in the shallows, then let me not pretend that these flounders are piranhas, still less sharks, and let me not overlook the hermit-crab, with his home on his back, or the plankton which is phosphorescing so prettily. And why not let them speak to me, in words which will be as old as the sand. And let me try and reply to them, though I don't yet have the tongue.

Friday 8 December

In the middle of the night reach out behind me – realise what I'm doing only well after I've done it – grab Eve's body and pull it up next to me. For a short span she's a man and (s)he's going to penetrate me from behind.

"I could buy an apparatus," Eve whispers.

Awake later with a sore throat, convinced I've caught some bug. Thoughts of the <u>tordi</u> from all those years ago.

On the couch, regret again that my feelings for men have not, in 6 years, found more direct expression, remaining as friendships and close bonds (often with homosexual or bisexual men). The closet door is open, but I don't seem motivated to step out, despite being motivated to be motivated.

Then: "I know I pushed you in a corner when I told you to get rid of the ridiculous Adami painting and bring back the Balthus. I'm aware that your getting rid of the Adami, and <u>not</u> bringing back the Balthus, has probably got nothing to do with me, even if it was a canny way out of the corner. You remember the dream I had years back in which you're pissing in the corner of my new flat, spoiling it. Well, I've a new corner for you to piss in."

". . ."

"Here's the corner. You want, don't you, to surprise me in the last. But you've no idea how to. It wouldn't be your style to give me a big summing-up of the 6 years, explaining all the stages, but you're aware at this point that it's about the only thing capable of surprising me. You don't just want to be predictable, do you? In a script I could write by myself?"

"Hmmmm?"

"And I'm telling you, warning you if you prefer, that your silence is utterly predictable."

"Eh bien."

Sneak a peak at my watch: barely 20 minutes, the bastard! Just because I shoved him in a pissy corner!

On the way out, ask him when he takes his break for Christmas. He tells me he'll work up to Saturday the 23rd. Confirm with him that our last session will, therefore, be on Friday the 22nd.

When I started analysis I didn't have too many hopes that it would make my life more stable, or even more straightforward. As for "happy", this had always seemed a self-defeating goal since by aiming at it you're almost bound to miss it. It was probably just as well my hopes weren't pinned to such masts. For it wasn't just my brain I'd find myself losing. I also abruptly lost my girlfriend, Trinh, the greater part of my composure, then a whole host of interests and abilities.

If these were the conditions, though, I accepted them (with much gnashing of teeth and whining). I accepted them because I was determined to go the whole way, whatever that meant, even if it meant letting go of all and sundry, to find myself afresh, speaking in a *new voice*. I'd know when that new speaking began, for then flesh and word would finally be one, and I'd be speaking where my body was.

Or, more simply, I'd have learned to use my tongue.

The first thing Eve said to me when at last we were alone together, after many months of café conversations, gazing mystified at each other, battling (she) with a post-divorce depression, and struggling (I) with an age-old need to mourn – we're on the beach at Cabourg, where I've invited her for the weekend, and the first thing she says to me, we've never so much as held hands, and she says to me: "Give me your tongue!"

She might as well have asked Achilles to give her his heel.

I gave to her, that weekend, as many bits of myself as I was able – as many "lengths" as the Scottish slang has it, blending wisdom and cringe. But I still have to doubt if I really gave her my tongue.

The flesh was willing – thank God for such not-so-small mercies. But the voice was weak. And the words of love remained to me the most foreign of the foreign. And so even the flesh had its weakness, precisely where the words had to form – the tongue, not to mention the lips and mouth. Kissing, never mind *French* kissing, was my *point faible*, not to say my *dénouement*, not to say my *nemesis* – I can't even find a decently English-sounding expression for my degree of incompetence!

Saturday 9 December

The strike goes on. I'm hoping it finishes on the day of my very last session. Fantasies of omnipotence: here I am orchestrating the French government, unions, economy. Six sessions left, a miserable 6 sessions to sum up 6 years.

Sum up: no getting away from the fact that there should be some sort of conclusion or report, some bilan the French would say. Some summation. "Off with his head!" would suffice, as it did for young Julien. And come to think of it, a Sergeant's "Off with his head!" would surely have some effect on my throat and voice.

"I'm pregnant," comes the chirp on the other end of the line.

For a second I think it's Eve. Am I appalled or delighted? Gulp.

"I'm so glad for you," I finally get out, when I've figured out it's Justine. What on earth am I up to? Their voices don't sound even remotely similar. "Big congratulations."

Then, as she's telling me all about it, a little imp working within me, anxiety ever ready to raise its pecker that I'm an incubus fertilising women as they sleep. It forces me to say: "You mean, all this just because I've been sleeping in your bed?"

Fortunately, she takes the joke.

Later, sitting in the building site, trying to keep warm enough to read the second of those books for review, by Alexakis. Take the chance to consult my old pal, the OED.

Cease: to stop, give over, discontinue, desist, to come to the end or to an intermission of a state or condition of 'being, doing, or suffering'

Conclude: to close any transaction, to end, to wind up, finish, to arrive by reasoning at a judgement or opinion, to draw an inference, deduce

End: to carry through to the end, finish, complete, conclude, come to a termination

Finish: to bring to an end, go through the last period or stage, bring to completion, make or perform completely

Interrupt: to break in upon, break the continuity of (something) in time, break off, make an interval or breach between the parts of (something continuous)

Don't bother to look up "leave", what Hamlet's not so great at (so that even Imperious Caesar comes back, "turned to clay"). Wonder if the French would be "quitter" or "partir". You "quitter" transitively (a place, a person), you "partir" intransitively.

"I'd like a selection of all of the above, please."

The man in the Word Shop looks bemused.

"Since all these words have something to offer me in my present situation."

He doesn't respond, so I go back to the Alexakis novel. Some problem here, and similar to the problem in the novel by the Russian, Makine. Not just that he's wavering between two countries, France and Greece. Something about the form. All these memories, with no necessary guidelines about what to include or exclude. That's not quite it either, but I'm on its tracks — hoping not just on my own tracks.

What did I tell the Sergeant yesterday? Heard him writing. Thank God I got it out:

"Either you are writing about me, in which case, believe me, I have every right to write about you."

He is still.

"Or you're not writing about me, you're writing your tax forms or love letters. In which case, given what I'm paying you, I have even more right to write about you!"

"Hmmmm!" (His most affirmative sort of "Hmmmm!")

There are ways and there are ways of bringing word and body together. Not all of them are joyful, and I'd had my share of the unfortunate kind before I started my analysis. One incident in particular stood as emblematic of how it was before I went to see the Sergeant, and it was often in my mind during these final weeks. It occurred in the spring of 1989 when I was visiting Bologna and was invited to dine at the house of Paula, a friend I'd made the year before. Everyone told me what an excellent cook she was, and so I didn't eat anything all day, to create room for whatever she'd feed me.

There's a wonderful *tortellini in brodo* as *primo*, accompanied by a fine Nebbiolo. This is followed by a brief pause before Lucia brings out what she tells me is a local speciality, a recipe dating from the sixteenth century. She goes into the kitchen, I hear the oven door opening, and when she comes back she's carrying an enormous dish on which are sitting what look to me like twenty blackbirds, with their heads still on.

Lucia must have seen my face – the face of one who has always delighted in songbirds – because she says, misinterpreting me completely: "Don't worry, I never buy poultry which has been raised in a battery, I only ever buy wild game".

In other words, just yesterday these little songsters were freely chirping their hearts out.

"They're *tordi*," she tells me. She doesn't know the French or English name.

The evening's a long one, with my stomach turning and the twitter of birdsong in my head. When I get home to where I'm staying, and check "tordi" in the dictionary, I'm sure I'm going to throw up. But no, I manage to keep the birds down. I even get to sleep that night, and only feel mildly guilty the next morning when woken by the song outside my window. All in all I'm pretty pleased with myself.

But when I'm going to the toilet two days later, I let out a yelp. It feels like I'm passing acid. I've not been exposed to any risk of infection in the past few months. So what can it be? I pull back the foreskin, look more closely.

What the fuck is that?

What indeed but a virulent and alarming dose of *tordi* – that is to say a dose of thrush.

Word and body, body and word: a bad joke of which I was the butt (or dick). And a translator in there too, working out connections which did not so much as occur to the rest of me. I thought of writing to the makers of Canesten, with which I salved the stinging, to ask if there were a prize for unusual ways of catching a dose.

I cycled frenetically round the Paris pavements and boulevards, wondering if anything had changed. The colitis had gone, the throat rarely bothered me now. But surely there must be some more gains, could I but focus upon them. However, when I tried to concentrate, all I could think of was bed, Justine's, or anyone else's, it didn't matter, lying down upon it, and not getting up for a week (except for the final sessions). I'd be so spectacularly ill that my excuse would be watertight, it'd let me get off the whirligig and stay put.

I pleaded to the germs to enter me and lay me low. But they avoided me as if it were I who were the plague, and left me the ironic epitome of rosy-cheeked energy and health.

"All that cycling must be doing you good," Eve told me. "You're looking better than I've ever seen you."

When I wondered what had changed, therefore, I wasn't able to affirm that I was any more in control of my body. Perhaps it was more in control of me? What I found, in any case, once I'd accepted that I couldn't oblige myself by falling ill, was an intimation of what *my body* would soon be losing – the voice and its words were more obvious – when I ceased to visit the Sergeant.

Psychoanalysis, if only in the most everyday of senses, is a very physical experience. For six years, three times a week, that journey to the island, the walk up those steps. Sometimes the walk was not so easy, such as when I had an infected ingrown toenail (helpful as ever, the Sergeant reminded me that "Oedipus" means "swollen foot"), or had twisted my knee in my dance class.

And soon I'd no longer be lying there with my legs raised, rubbing the bald patch on his wall, watching the cracks grow on his ceiling (warning him it might soon fall in, as mine had recently done). No more rushing to the bank machine to get out two hundred and fifty francs, no more stuffing them in my pocket in order to hand them to him at the end. No more glancing up at the Francis Bacon on the way out.

Word and body, body and word. Being unable to bring them together even in my imagination, let alone in reality, I rehearsed rituals I knew my body would soon be missing. And from those rehearsals a question sprang and snapped at me with worrying jaws: How would he say goodbye to me, that final time? And how would he close the door?

I was so alarmed by the snapping of these questions, which all of a sudden seemed so urgent, that I had to get off my bicycle, dash into the nearest café, and rush to the toilet. Yet when I got there nothing happened. I was only searching for the memory of an almost forgotten leaky bowel.

Sunday 10 December

Eve's for lunch, en route to the building site. Desserts from Stohrer, the best patisserie in Paris. But I'm just cracking the crystallised sugar on top of their famous puits d'amour when Eve pushes it away from me.

"Careful now," she scoffs, "wouldn't like you to fall into the well of love."

I sit there frustrated and abject. "I think I'm doing my bit. I'm trying at least."

"Very trying."

"That's not fair, and it's not original either."

"Every gesture you make, of friendship, every franc you lend me or gift you offer —"

"— And don't forget" (I know the song) "don't forget every penis I erect and sustain."

"They're all just compensation for what you're unable or unwilling to do: look me in the eyes, kiss me on the mouth, and tell me you love me."

Sure, there's something too absolute in what she says. I'm waiting for her to tell me that the Amazonian rainforest is being decimated, and that the pandas are refusing to mate in Edinburgh Zoo, all because of my amorous inhibitions. And then, she shouldn't take it so personally, since I've always been like this, and it's always been lamented — though with what scraps of brain remain, I decide this would not be a compliment, and so keep it to myself. I scowl at the old excuse I used to furnish, years back, about how the rites of love have been banalised by the times, by too many bad books and films — Woody Allen's "I luff you" in Annie Hall.

In short, I'm dumbfounded.

For despite the fact that the pandas would still refuse to mate, rainforests would be destroyed, despite Hollywood with its dreary sentimentality and Mantovani with his Thousand Strings, despite the fact that nothing lasts anyway, and that life will go on distributing its disappointments, false-diarrhoeas, and dybbuks — despite all this, Eve is probably right. As far as I'm concerned at least, which is more than far enough. All sentimentality aside: I am less than human.

But God, how am I meant to attend to my inhumanity with the water pouring in from upstairs?

Get on with my work, and set my end-of-semester exams. Choose some passages for commentary from the texts I've taught this semester. Get lost again in Lolita, waste an hour, snap out of it, tell myself that most of the novel is bravura, show-off stuff, and cruel to boot and icy-cold. But then read, of Humbert Humbert's wife, Lolita's mother:

> We had highballs before turning in, and with their help, I would manage to evoke the child while caressing the mother. This was the white stomach within which my nymphet had been a little curved fish in 1934. This carefully dyed hair, so sterile to my sense of smell and touch, acquired at certain lamplit moments in the poster bed the tinge, if not the texture, of Lolita's curls.

Think, idiotically, since no one is about to give me any such choice: if I could, by papal decree, be ordained with the ability to love like a human, and speak it to a real, loveable, palpable, passionate, supple, stretchy, woman – such a one as Eve – who formerly adored me and into whose curves I fit so snugly; or be allowed to write a few lines of comparable beauty; which would I choose? I would choose – "thinking of aurochs and angels", as Lolita ends, "the secret of durable pigments, prophetic sonnets, the refuge of art".

What an inhuman wretch I am. It's just as well no pontiff's about to offer me that choice. Nabokov: a genius wretch. And myself: just wretch.

But enough of self-aggrandisement and auto-flagellation. Get on with that TLS review. The next few days will only be getting busier, and I've not yet mastered the technique of writing while I pedal.

I'd written often enough for my editor at the *TLS* to know I could rely on him to take the awkwardness off whatever I sent, with a bit of what he called "nip and tuck". However, since he was so acute, I worried he'd call me up, after I'd faxed the review of those two books, and say: "But I asked you for a review, not an autobiography, still less an account of the end of your analysis!"

No complaint forthcoming, however, just a message on the answering-machine a couple of days later, saying that the review had arrived and seemed fine.

The review started:

> Both prize-winning works, *La Langue maternelle* and *Le Testament français*, purport to be novels, though they come on strongly, unashamedly indeed as memoirs, reminiscences, autobiographies. Both are by "foreigners" who have sought to escape their homelands into France, and who have written their tributes to their *pays d'élection* in French. The two novels chart the workings of memory transplanted to foreign soil and fertilised by foreign customs, syntax and vocabulary.

As the review continued, I expected my editor to add: "And what's all this about shit? I thought you'd given up on tributes to colon and cloacum!"

> Curiously, there is a single memory common to the two works. It is of how, in the past, dogs' excrement was collected and then sold to be used in tanneries to soften the skins.

The review went on to summarise the scant plot of *La Langue maternelle*. But when I tried to round it off with a critique of the novel's final pages, the voice in my head was back, more querulous than ever: "Since when have conclusions and their necessities, or lack thereof, been so important to you?"

I tried to appease the voice in my head by repeating the dictum about how literary criticism is *always* disguised autobiography. Yet this can cut two ways. Either I was confusing the book under review with my own life, and imputing to it my own desire to find a necessary form for the last six years. Or – and I pinned my colours to this mast – my own concerns were so close to those of the book under review, not only through my experience of foreignness and French but also through my very desire to wring some necessity out of the last few years, that I had a privileged insight into the unsuccessful short-cuts which such desire can lead to.

I put aside the review and went back to my journal.

Big dreams? Little dreams? I was looking for a necessity to emerge from the final weeks of the analysis, with an optimism as unwarranted as it was insistent. And I'd begun looking for something similar in my journal, in what it might become. Yet without short-cuts and sleights-of-hand, I knew it would be hard. What these two novels tried, in an unsuccessfully Proustian way, was to meld the life into the work, such that "autobiography" and "fiction" would become irrelevant distinctions. If I were to try a comparable "melding", wouldn't this consist in conveniently eroding the distinction between my analysis and the rest of my life?

The long scar on my face started to sting, reminding me of the limits of analysis and interpretation.

Even now, with the end fast approaching, I couldn't bear to turn my whole life, still less my writing, still less writing in general, into a reflection of my psychic or psychosomatic processes. Nor, *pace* my scar – and this realisation filled me with boundless gratitude – nor had the Sergeant ever tried to make me do so. He had never tried, that is, to make analysis become the be-all or, crucially now, the *end*-all of life. Not even just of my life. He'd never attempted that sleight-of-hand to which I know analysts and therapists of certain persuasions are prone, by which what the patient says is taken to be a reflection on the person of the analyst or on the analytic situation (a sleight-of-hand which is usually called "interpretation of the transference"). I'd read numerous reports of such a way of proceeding, and the name of Melanie Klein often cropped up in this context. The patient might be speaking of a pair of old socks – but what did that say, or intend to say, about *your* (the patient's) hostility towards *me* (the analyst), or about *our* relationship?

Not once did the Sergeant imply that when I was speaking about my socks, or indeed about any of my smells or surrogates, I was really talking about him, about "our relationship", or even about analysis. (The closest he came was his joke about my wishing to be "Renato" – and that was precisely a joke.) Not once did he try to convince me that there was an "our" which might usefully qualify or permit the term "relationship". Of course I was on occasion doing precisely that, talking about what I fantasised of him or it. But rather than draw my attention to these fantasies of transference, he preferred to work through them. He never brought me up short with a reduction of the world to the tiny scope of his person. Nor did he inflate his own person, so that he could become commensurate with my fantasies. There's a simpler way of putting this: not once did he try to impose *his faith* upon me. Not once in these six years did he attempt what so-called "interpretation of the transference" is always intending to do: not once did he try to *convert* me.

My gratitude went out to the Sergeant for such tact (such ecumenism). Yet even as it did so, I could see that without such a sleight-of-hand, short-cut, or conversion, then for me to find a form for my big or little dreams I would probably have to be as clumsy as Gilhaney in *The Third Policeman* when he knocks the chests off the table, or as violent as Julien Sorel in *Le Rouge et le Noir* when he attempts by murder to become the subject of his own story.

Without faith and its ability to transmute base matter into gold then how could I hope to find necessity in analysis or recreate it on the page? Without faith and its power to subsume, then the world remained the world, analysis analysis, and the Sergeant was just a man in an armchair (a man with none of the allure of Lady Agnew of Lochnaw).

From this man I was determined, despite my gratitude for his tact, to extract some recognition and reassurance, even if it meant my doing a John Wayne and converting on my death bed.

Monday 11 December

Justine needs her bicycle back. She's sick of sitting stationary in her car polluting her embryo with car fumes from traffic jams. So I cycle from her flat to my own, go into my cellar, dig up my old racer, unridden for 10 years, pump up the tyres, adjust the brakes. (This bicycle was so much a part of me in my twenties that, like the characters in The Third Policeman, I risked becoming more bicycle than human.) Cycle to Justine's on her bicycle, guiding my own with my right hand, a delicate and exhausting balancing act, raising some cheers from the public – "Courage!", "Pas mal!" – which has been almost completely humanised by this strike. Go by way of the arsehole of Paris: Crimée, Ourq, the rear of the eerily silent Gare du Nord. Almost burst my lungs on the hill of rue du Crimée. Hand over bicycle. Race back to the ruin to pick up exams. Race on to work.

Step into the office of the department secretary at 1 minute to 4, exam due at 4, sweating, feet frozen, panniers falling off me. Ask him for the students' exam books. And though in the 3 years he has worked there I've never, not once, seen him do a stroke of work, he decides to announce to me, "You're late for your exam".

Think: But I haven't been late for a single class, despite the strikes, flat, snow, and slow punctures.

Think: the Glasgae kiss.

Think: of course not, stick to insults.

Think: No, not even that. Just stare at him, eyes narrowed, take the exam books, walk out, and slam his door as hard as I possibly can, so the whole building reverberates.

(Taking my revenge upon his door isn't innocent. Doors can be closed, and doors can be slammed – that includes the Sergeant's.)

Learn, later, that this is the secretary's last week at work (at "work"). Thank God I didn't miss my chance, however petty. Note this down on the pros list: increased ability, analysis assisting, to react in the moment (even if it took the Belleville bottle across my face to dispense for good with the softly-softly approach). What a saving on the bile of regrets.

What could the Sergeant say to satisfy my craving for an adequate conclusion?

Maybe it's not the answer that's lacking, but the question that's misguided. For any answer I can give would be mine, not his, so can't surprise me, just further etchings on his silence. I had to invent myself when I was too young, then re-invent myself too frequently. Though I've come up with all sorts of avatars, I long for someone to relieve me of that need to invent, and show me instead what I've inherited — a life, for example, to which I then have a right.

If I can't get at it directly, maybe I can get close by way of an analogy?

Let me try. (In any case it'll be fun to be writing more than just notes for once.)

For more than 10 years I've been taking the métro round Paris, which allows me to emerge at the station closest to my destination: Cité, for example, in the case of analysis, or Latour-Maubourg in the case of the university. I'm an expert at assembling complex routes which include the "fast métro" (the RER) and which let me go, say, from Les Halles to Courcelles by way of Étoile. And so experienced a traveller (or gofer) am I, and so efficient is the system, that I'm rarely more than a couple of minutes out in my estimate of the time it will take between any two Paris locations. It's a supremely rational, modern, and practical system, of which I've become a part.

But let me look at it more closely. Forget for the moment that there are strikes on, during which the system falls apart, as these normally tend to confirm how efficient and indispensable the system is when it comes back into operation.

Looked at more closely, what I have in fact assembled for myself is a series of discrete patches, connected by underground tunnels. Yet the distance between any two such patches is as long or as short as these tunnels (as the gofer burrows, not as the crow flies); while the areas falling between two patches, anything more than 200 yards from a métro, such as the space in the 5th arrondissement, or between Marx Dormoy and Crimée, remain sites of vague unease. And then, it's not just tunnel distance determining, but the number of changes too: so that two sites can be virtually adjacent, but if they require a change, they'll seem all-too-far apart; a double change virtually unthinkable. And so there are, I confess, acquaintances I hardly see from one year to the next because, though they don't live far from my flat, getting to their place requires me to change twice.

And then add to that the fact that I loathe certain métro stations: either for more or less rational reasons (the enormity of Montparnasse-Bienvenue, the filth of Barbès-Rochechouart, the piped music of Châtelet-les-Halles), or because of memories (the food poisoning at Glacière, the stop that led to the blood at Belleville, the sadness of the flea market at Mairie de Montreuil), or because I just don't like the sound (Ranelagh, Javel, again Marx Dormoy, and worst of all Ourq). Then add that some lines I prefer to others (line 4 is regular but stinks, line 8 screeches on the bends, RER C requires a wrestle to get the doors open, RER A is literally the busiest line in the world). And what we find emerging, in place of a highly efficient and rational system of automated locomotion, is a different sort of transport altogether, of "transfert" or "transference", this one chock-a-block with hobgoblins, rival tribes, fault rifts, to whose grid and coordinates I've been orienting my inner compass with an ever-increasing insistence and rigidity over the years.

And so the Sergeant's final gambit?

The Sergeant's final gambit would be like coming out of the métro and getting on my bike.

Suddenly the grid falls apart, and new circulation flows.

"Look," I'm continually saying to myself, "I can turn right here and get from Crimée to Ourq, which not only have I never done, but never even imagined."

I can still predict pretty accurately the time required to get from A to B, but on the way I don't have to breathe my neighbour's ill-digested garlic or fend off a pickpocket, I can inspect old streets in Ménilmontant, buildings only seen in guide books of the Quartier-Latin, watch an elderly lady leading a cat by a piece of twine on rue Myrrha. From Père-Lachaise to Voltaire becomes possible, and in a mere 6 minutes, where it would have been 8 stops and an unpleasant change. I can go and see the friends I've been neglecting, and just "pop in" (the very term has dropped out of my metropolitan's vocabulary). I can go north, south, east, or west-north-west. And while certain names retain their menace, since they're no longer destinations I glide past them, nodding as I go. Paris is small: no distance takes more than 40 minutes, and the time passes quickly when it's not measured in superstition and anxiety. "So that street's next to that! So from here you can see the rooftops!" And not only is a new fluid space being configured, but I'm not just sitting on my arse being led, am being active, getting there under my own steam, and my legs are stronger for it too.

And, yes, if the Sergeant were to make such a verbal-vélo gambit? Then what would I reply?

I'd reply, I suppose, "Well, Dr Sergeant, it's a lovely idea. But aren't you forgetting something?"

". . ."

"Lorries speeding in the slow lane. Cars so impatient. Pernod-drunk drivers. Mesdames in a rush. And the odd criminal — such a one as I might just be — who actually wants to run you down!"

Putting my mouth where my money was: I'd been trying to do it for long enough.

Only, now what changed was that I realised I couldn't add up many clear instances of *mouth*, whereas the total *money* I had to try actively to ignore. While waiting in the cubicle before going in, I found myself wondering what else I could have done with it all, or what I would have done with it, say, had I lived a hundred years ago (a habit of imagining picked up in history classes as a child).

Historical relativism wasn't new to me, but now it showed its teeth. Psychoanalysis was so recent a practice. And while I didn't go so far as to consider my symptoms the direct products of psychoanalysis (in the way that Marx considers criminals the products of the Law), I did think they might have been as well addressed, had I lived back then, at a brothel, say, or in church.

It wasn't hard, with all the plush around me, and the drapery, to muse myself into what the French used to call a "maison close". I could have invited Eve along for a threesome. Or I might have met a Baudelaire, waiting in line, or a Proust, had I sprouted a taste for working-class lads. Or I'd surely have found some other outlet back then, slaughtering natives of some African tribe, say, or constructing bridges – Robert Louis lighthouses! – or, for that matter, rustling sheep across the border from England, all of which would have been considerably more exciting. And even the brothel wouldn't have stung me as hard as the Sergeant.

Psychoanalysis had come, and psychoanalysis would go, while the route to its verities would become overgrown with ferns and bushes, until it could no longer be found. (I had a counter-argument, but had to delay it to inspect my metaphor, which seemed to be suggesting more than I'd intended of what Uncle Toby in *Tristram Shandy* calls the "covered way".) But all truths being subject to such conditions of relativity, of context and erosion, then relativism itself had to be relativised. And a truth *for now* would, if *dear* enough, be more than sufficient for me.

How dear was *dear*?

Since psychoanalysis could come and go, but money just seemed to *go*, and since nothing my mouth mouthed seemed to win any of it back, then as dear as the hole which this relativism was burning in my pocket, which made its contents fall out, straight into the Sergeant's coffers.

Tuesday 12 December

"Eve says to me: 'You've been in analysis for 6 years but you still don't know how to kiss me and tell me you love me'."

Hope as I lie down on the couch that this opening thrust may provoke him, but it doesn't come out as portentous as intended. With the result that I imagine a subsequent conversation in the accents of two nattering Scottish wifeys ("So she sais to me" – "Well you gis tael hir fray me"). While the Sergeant not only declines to stick up for me by praising my amorous expansiveness, he doesn't stick up for anyone at all, not even for himself, just his usual ". . .".

"It's not sex, as such, thank God, dieu merci, and fondle lots of wood. It's much more perilous than that. For me at least. And I'm sick of it – with it. Sick."

"You wish me to megalene?"

Add to my surprise that he's uttered, his deep smoker's voice, his thickish accent, and I have to ask him to repeat himself. "What was that?"

"You wish me to intervene?"

"Yehh!" If I had my schoolboy's cap on, I'd toss it in the air, shout "Hurrah!"

". . ."

"Call that intervention?"

The rescue not arriving, I wait and wait. Then: "Take her away from me – Eve and all the rest – and make her, make them, yours. And you'll have to share her with other men too, since she'll soon wear you out. But if she belongs to several it'll only increase my security – recall the Roberta solution."

"What are you afraid of?"

"Choking, suffocating. Goes back, like my eating problems, to before my father's death, I feel as if someone were about to roll over in bed and smother me. But my father's death gives an extra weight, extra smother, with the threat of a corpse on top of me. I want to get up, out, away, then I realise I haven't even escaped from bed. Again and again and again."

I try to focus, silently, upon that suffocation I have never, for panic, allowed to come over me. I'd rather put up with fearsome solitude in its place. If I could emerge, there would be — would be — a woman before me, and I would speak to her. There would be no third person. Time would have stopped. And it would only start to move again when I saw him at the door, come to lead this woman away. Only then would my terror abate and let me breathe again.

"If I were to say 'I love you', I'd be betraying."

"Betraying whom?"

Think: my father? my mother? But neither feels correct.

Then words and image fade, and it's my nose working, as it inhales a woman's perfume. Confused, I look round. There's nothing to see. If there'd been a heavily perfumed woman prior to me on the couch I'd have smelt her, with my bloodhound nose, the moment I walked in.

Then, of a sudden, I'm seated in my parents' bedroom, with the big double bed, the wardrobe with its sliding concertina door. I can even take time to admire the late 1950s light-fittings. Here they are too, though I only see my father's back, dressed in a dinner jacket. My mother getting into a ballgown. And I'm proud of them, they look so elegant and smart and sexy. I open my mother's alligator-skin handbag, put my head down, and inhale the leather and scent. They are going out, but I am going with them in my thoughts.

Some day I too shall be big.

"Pah! But I'll never be as big as they were, even if .— horror — I'm already their age. And it wouldn't just be one of them or the other I'd be betraying, not a person at all, but a hope, theirs, and a passion, add to it an era too, why not, not just theirs or mine but a real era, when people still believed, got married, wore dinner jackets and ballgowns without irony or shame."

". . ."

By speaking, I obliterate the memory, if memory it was, and my parents have vanished.

"Happily ever after."

"Hmmmm?"

"If I could be one of the two, like him or like her, then how would I know that this happiness could stop? Panics me no end – no end – that it might go on for ever, that the present bliss, were I to kiss, say, kiss and say – would last for ever. Yet I know it makes no sense, because only then would the possibility come of a real ending, for I should at last, at last, have <u>begun</u>."

"Eh bien!" And very abruptly too, not quite interrupting me, but certainly not letting me get another word in edgeways.

On the stairs check the watch: 30 minutes. Bless the strikes. For there was no one after me, I'm sure of it. So for once the timing wasn't contingent.

Countdown: 5 sessions left.

Like anyone else who has been in therapy or analysis, and like many who have been in extensive medical treatment, I heard a voice inside me – mine spoke in dourest Scots – which told me there was nothing wrong here that a "guid day's work would no put right". What was changing now was the tense: there *had been* nothing wrong with me that a guid day's work *would no hae* put right. I sometimes tried to silence that voice by pretending I only spoke French. Here in France, I responded (through some translator), psychoanalysis is very much part of the culture, as is hypochondria, ever since Molière's day, witness. the fact that you can't travel a block in Paris without encountering a pharmacy.

I'd be about to add a Gallic sneer and raise the cockerel above my head, when, to my shame, I'd spot the billboard. There it was, whether advertising the discount store called Darty, or Hippo restaurants where the steaks are enormous, or Papal tours where entrance to the Vatican is free, or Crud toilet cleaner which has twice the shit-cleaning coverage –

there it was, the Scotsman in his kilt, or the refrigerator, or the Hippo, the Pope, or the toilet bowl. No indignity was spared my national costume, in the endeavour to get the cut-price equation across: Scotsman equals meanness.

When I went back to pondering the historical or cultural relativities, it was my own Scots voice I was hearing, no Gallic insouciance, as it counted the pennies or francs which were emptying thrice weekly from the pocket or sporran. I was giving my money away. My hard-earned money? There'd been fifteen years of fairly arduous study to get to where I was (I momentarily overlooked the fact that I *enjoyed* my current job). And most of it had been financed by the Scottish Education Department, which meant that the honest sodality of Scottish taxpayers had been indirectly subsidising my analysis. Giving it away, though it was far from unlimited; the better, as I thought, to give myself away – there mouth where money.

Hoping perhaps, the voice asked, that you'd become so much poorer, so damned *indigent* (Beckett's word), that what would remain would be your body and its few essential words?

Yes, these words, by their very scarcity, would *become* me – in at least two senses of "become". The remaining words would *fetch* me, be *fetching*.

With the countdown well under way, I consoled myself with the fact that the Sergeant hadn't raised the fee since I started. Then I told myself that seven hundred and fifty francs a week didn't mean the same now as it had in 1990, and that in real terms the sessions were now cheaper. It's true, I was probably earning less now than then – as I made a point of explaining to him – since there'd been a pay freeze at the university. But this was all my side, when the money was something between us.

I didn't need to worry about the Sergeant being unable to pay his bills. He might not have a Courbet, but he could sell the Bacon, and that would see him through a good few years. His wealth was in fact one of the things that drew me to him from the start, *endeared* me to him. Not so much because I hoped for some of it to rub off on me, more because it signalled his *independent means*.

I paid him, paid him every session, but since to the constant fee contrasted my ever-increasing need to speak without interference (something like the kind of interference picked up on a radio), I did sometimes wonder if I should not be paying him more, if only to ensure he needed me less and less – less than ever.

But then I heard a chuckle – not mine this time but the Sergeant's – which seemed to ask me who I was trying to kid. For I'd had my chance to pay more, and I'd cannily avoided it.

I, the chancer, looking back in my journal for the entry on that franc-saving day six years before.

26 March 1990

My self-imposed rule about not reporting here anything said in the sessions – does it extend to discussions of money? No one but myself to give the answer, and I'm not sure.

When we were fixing a price, back when I started just over a month ago – seems so much longer – he said his rate was 300 francs a session. I told him I couldn't afford to come twice a week at that price – and I genuinely meant it – and beat him down to 250.

Took me only a fortnight to realise that twice weekly, Tuesdays and Fridays, wasn't enough. Would have to stretch my wallet, take on some extra work, translations, whatever.

Today, steeling my Scottish nerve, after the session I say: "I've been thinking that Tuesdays seem a long way from Fridays. That if you had a space I'd like to come three times a week."

He looks sceptical.

"So I would pay you 750 francs a week."

I try to keep a straight face. Then it's his face which cracks, as he starts to chuckle, and goes on laughing for quite some time – not a scoff or a guffaw, more as if he were laughing at himself for having been out-manoeuvred. Or just laughing at the vagaries of life – even life in analysis.

He scrutinises his agenda, and offers me Wednesdays at 1.00 p.m.

I accept, breathe a sigh of relief.

※

Why did I always make a point of handing him the notes after every single session? Was it to remind me how I was paying up front? To help him fiddle his taxes? Or was it not, rather, to be continually reminding us both of this jolly March day?

What's certain is that even at discount rate I paid a lot of money, and *spent* a lot of time.

"For what?" Eve kept pestering me. "For what?"

Fortunately, there were a few ready answers.

For his time, since he spent that too, even if the variable length broke down any strict money–time equivalence. For the assurance that he'd be there, and not cease to be there; even if, again, this had the limitations which I pointed out to him. For the right that he *not* become a friend, for the right as it were never to employ the first person plural pronoun or possessive, never to say "We" or "Our". For a great deal of silence, of course, as well as the right to be very stupid, to cast off whole ladlefuls of nous. For the right, too, not to care a toss about what he might want, or even *be*, outside the confines of the sessions.

Ready answers, these. Not quite obscuring another answer, which showed itself dimly, in the distance. By squinting, and raising my hand to shade my eyes, I began to make it out.

What?

That by paying him so diligently, never missing a session or asking for an advance, I had bought myself the right to attempt to betray him. I had put my confidence in him (following Joe Mantegna's terms in David Mamet's film). But then, by accepting all my money, he had also put his in me. And now the con-trick could work both ways. Only – and I settled into this paradox as into one of my favourite bramble bushes – by paying him all that cash (to keep quiet and the rest) I was also ensuring that it would be extremely hard to exert my right to betray his confidence, commit a crime against him. For what did I have of his to betray? What of his could I sell?

It occurred to me that I could molest his wife on the stairs, or I could kidnap his child (until I remembered that I didn't know where the happy family dwelt). Or make off with one of his paintings – the Bacon would do nicely. But whenever I imagined these scenes of theft and revenge, I'd see him shaking his head, gesturing me back towards the couch, rather as he had when I'd asked him about the rules for ending analysis.

Once I'd scratched myself thoroughly in my bramble bush with my thrashing around for an idea, I'd indulge in the balm of mental shopping. Seven hundred and fifty francs a week made three thousand a month (virtually four hundred pounds), and I wouldn't fritter it all away on telephone bills or the repairs my flat would need if ever I won my court case and got the neighbours to mend their shower. No, I'd buy myself some luxury every month, confident that when the time came – it was less than two weeks away, and my budget would feel the benefits by Christmas – I'd think of some appropriate objects or events.

The balm of shopping worked. I felt calm enough to ask myself again what I had of his that I could possible betray or sell.

And this time something did occur to me: his *silence*.

Wednesday 13 December

So there's a real prospect of the strikes coming to an end. Only hope of chaos now, if that happens, is a freak snowstorm followed by a chill. Do my Chris Bonnington impersonation, and hope for a reaction as I climb into his office wearing crampons.

On the couch, the dream: "So I'm standing next to Justine, when we suddenly realise we desire one another, and I realise our desire is lesbian, for I know I am in fact a woman."

Shit, I'm off on the wrong foot. I'm a woman because I feel it, not because I know it.

"Hmmmm?"

"I kiss Justine, and it's a real kiss, sighing, and I feel myself start to moisten inside — not stiffen, moisten. I picture our two bodies entwined naked together, and I can't tell which is hers, which mine. Feel guilty because I know she fancies my friend Matthew.

"'That's irrelevant,' she tells me, 'because he's a man and you're a woman. Okay, he's bisexual, but he's still a man.'

"Though I've often enough dreamed what it might be like to be a woman, never before have I been one so fully, internally, organically.

"We walk together, trying to find a place to lie down, and our legs are heavy with lust. We enter a house whose door is standing open, go upstairs, but all the rooms are occupied."

Who are in these rooms, I wonder? Take a guess — no one's going to correct me: "Two brothers in two rooms, one of whom is me, the male me. We leave the house, Justine and I, enter an auditorium-style lecture-hall, and she tells me, 'We must do it here, now!' But the hall is filling up, and I'm left with just the longing to kiss again — yes, kiss! We're out on the street, this time in a bus queue. Then Matthew appears, looking wasted as if he's been up all night, unshaven, weight of the world — the man's world — on his shoulders. Wonder if he will recognise me now I'm a woman."

Think: a woman, yes, but without a sex change. No words for that, none that I can think of at least.

"Just before Matthew reaches us, a number 4 bus comes along, and Justine and I get on it, relieved. Sure we're at last on our way to safety and sex."

"Number 4?" asks the Sergeant. I'd been listening to him as I talked, scribbling away.

"The number — 4 — is how many sessions I have left with you once this session is over."

He is quiet for some seconds, no scribbling, and then I hear him rise to his feet.

"Eh bien."

Forget — forget? — to look at my watch on the way out.

"Putting my mouth where my money was" raised questions about my *mouth*, of course, about my voice, and about my *money* too, necessarily. But it also raised questions about exactly what was implied by the *my*; questions which, far from being resolved in these final sessions of analysis, were now pinching me mercilessly. For if there was complete confusion over gender, then what did it mean to say "*my* mouth"? Clearly something new, since with that mouth I could kiss, and how.

Six years of analysis, and a quantity of money I dared not yet calculate, and all this to discover that I was in fact a lesbian. And that as such I could finally say "my mouth" with something like a sense of possession, and so be able to give it away.

It wasn't that I objected to my new lesbian status, only what was I meant to *do* with it? Whatever there was in my dream-lust for Justine that caught my longing for a sister, there didn't seem much I could do with that either. I'd already figured out what a sister might have offered: the girly things, the magazines and jewellery and perfumes, the soiled knickers and open bathroom doors by which my male friends were tormented by their older sisters. I'd even come to accept that in my yearning for feminine beauty there existed scant desire to "possess" the woman who appeared to contain or embody it, in the way I "possessed" Eve (possessing nothing), but a desire rather to possess it *as* a woman (or where that was impossible then as a woman possesses another woman).

My mouth. *My* mouth!

With such confusion reigning, when I couldn't even make up my mind about my gender, did I really expect to find something as private as orifice and as public as cash coming together?

What a right royal mess.

Nor was this the end of the confusion. For if gender was one hurdle, then it wasn't the only one. The white blobs had descended from off the scree slope in the distance, and they were making their way towards me.

The landscapes of my dreams, which analysis dusted off and polished, may have come down to me from some Clan Gunn memory-bank, but if so then the memories were post-Clearances, for the hillsides and moors were dispeopled.

Oh, but they weren't devoid of life. I'd climb a fence, and there, being blown gently by the melancholy wind, was a tuft of wool. Or, leaping from clod to clod across a peat bog, I'd stop to inspect a white sun-baked skeleton or skull. And then there was a sudden dash from close to me, startled and foolish. And the surprise wasn't one-sided. For if I was always startling sheep in my dreams, then they were always finding and startling me – and not only in my dreams.

I had problems enough over gender. But add to these a confusion over *genus*!

Thursday 14 December
Morning

"Wouldn't you like to come to Scotland with me for Christmas?"

"What's the point in that? Since you're going on to Italy."

"I think it might be fun. Who knows what I'll be like when the analysis is over."

"Make your mind up first about what you're leaving behind, what you're going towards."

"There might be snow, firesides, sh–"

Left holding the receiver, with the drone-tone where Eve should be.

Until this analysis is over I've nothing more to offer. At the same time my "countdown" is making every contact overdramatic — can't even say "countdown" without sounding ridiculous, since it leads to blast-off, lift-off. A quite inappropriate phallic spurt, where I'm going out with more of a Sapphic sigh than a priapic bang.

Evening

Stubborn is my middle name. Just after that conversation I go out and buy Eve an Air France ticket for Edinburgh. Not that I anticipate feeling lonely in Scotland — on the contrary, I'm longing to lose myself in the hills, hopes of snow. But I want her to share that light with me, those mountains — those sheep.

Trying to correct exams, thinking about how the Sergeant isn't doing a thing to help me find a subject for what to write next. I tell him I see it as a new setting-forth. But there's got to be more to it than my botched Robert Louis Stevenson impersonation.

Given the Sergeant says nothing, I try to use the sessions to do the work myself. But the mind goes blank, like a whiteout. Stay with this whiteness, expecting an image or word to emerge, if not a fully fledged idea or narrative. But then, instead of that, it's a 10-franc coin I hear drop in the analytic metre as another chunk of silence passes by.

How much did I just get for that 10 francs? 25 minutes average = 250 francs = 10 francs a minute. Jesus! That's more than a pound a minute!

Outrageous!

Why have I never thought of it in these terms before? Why, it's a crime, it's downright daylight robbery!

"I'm being robbed!"

Hear him shift in his chair, move his papers around in a way that convinces me he's elsewhere. He's reading the letters he received today, or some new learned article. Imagine it to be Freud's "Analysis Terminable and Interminable". Or he's got his nose in January's issue of Marie Claire (out already).

Fat chance of getting to the bottom of my endeavours to find a "voice", when my attempt was being upstaged by sheep and their bleats. Fat chance or slim, the closer the end approached, the more intently I concentrated on whether, if not my speaking voice, then at least my writing voice had, over the six years, become any more "my own".

If more, which was debatable, then was this not just the effect of the change in age and the accumulation of experience? Was it not just another proof of the lack of a scientific "control"? When I failed to answer these questions, a sort of blankness or whiteness came over me again. I tried to project the question into the future, wondering what I could possibly write next.

Outside of the sessions, where there were no 10-franc coins going clunk, when I tried to peer into the blank canvas of my Triptych Part III, I'd find myself drifting into thoughts of what the Sergeant had said about the left-hand panel, which he had read (or which I had at least given him), or about the right-hand one, about which I had prattled incessantly through 1994, or indeed about the fact of their joint *ovinicity*.

Others – friends, colleagues, editors, even some unknown readers who'd written letters – had been loquacious with suggestions and interpretations: My writing was about recovery of the past, about the course of my psychoanalysis, about the mind/body split, about the idea of "translatability", and even was part of a Grail quest, yet to be completed. And of the sheep, that they represented Scotland, they embodied Eve or my father; the sheep were language, were "interculturality", were animal life as opposed to human. It was even suggested, I suppose it was inevitable, that they were Our Saviour Jesus Christ.

All of which suggestions were welcome, and all of which I allowed to amble over the blankness, waiting for the interpretation from the one who'd be able to say something more persuasive, if only because he'd been paid for precisely that.

What *did* the Sergeant say about my writing and its sheep?

". . ."

Not a single word. Not one bleeding word, unless you count the "Merci" when I handed him the published copy of *Almost You*.

Rien.

Nihil.

Nyet.

His silence gathered together all the friendly, wise, considered interpretations within its blankness, rounded up the more wayward suggestions too, and then, as if by covering them all in snowflakes, made them disappear.

Friday 15 December

Not changed my clothes in days, since they're all at the ruin, and when I get there on the bike it's too cold to think of undressing. The showman pulls back the curtain, stares at me like I'm a tramp.

Every night a dream, made to analytic measure. Last night's:

"So it's Justine again. I'm in her country house, in the kitchen, and she's baking, a woman in her home."

Thoughts of how I used to sit watching my mother baking scones, on a shelf from which I could also keep an eye on what was happening outside in the street. The men are out at school or work, but I'm still too young.

"I look through the windows onto Justine's garden, they're French windows. Learnt what that meant when I was small, windows you could walk through, like magic."

Hear the Sergeant scribbling.

"Suddenly, outside, see a little monkey — you little monkey! It wants to come in, and Justine tells me to let it, though it troubles me. And it's followed by one, then two, then more, bigger and blacker, menacing with huge ungainly testicles. They're all male — no, they're all mâle — so it's the mâle-mal, the male-evil that's invading, and by every aperture and orifice, climbing the walls, hanging from the ceiling, while Justine continues her baking, unperturbed."

Out of breath — that alarm again.

"J'essaie de les bloquer avec un tabouret. No, in English, I try to block their passage — with a stool!"

Tension drops. I can't help snickering. Faint echo from behind the couch.

"Hmmmm." (That's me for once.) "Anyway, stool or no stool, I know I'm not going to keep them out."

Rather anticlimactic ending.

Try to pick myself up. But this dream makes me feel as if I'm a lexicographer about to complete a dictionary who's just discovered a new letter. Here I am, trying to finish, busy being rogered by monkeys through French windows, hoping to keep them out with shit.

"It should mean I'm trying to keep Mummy for myself, but it doesn't feel like that. Because when I mention the kitchen I become it, I'm wholly it, with a w, and h-o-l-y too, I guess, full of holes and sacred. And here's the monkeys trying to penetrate my female space, and it's no fun, let me tell you — a pain in the arse!"

Wonder, for a second, if my mother wanted me a girl-child. But she's always maintained she wanted boys, not girls.

"For once I'm in the perfect space from which to watch the world, warm inside and secure, but curious about what's going on beyond. As a child I'd sit on that kitchen shelf and watch the neighbours, their cats, the bicycles, a football rolling down the road. I knew them all. For once I was neither keeping the world at arm's length nor absorbing it into me. La juste distance. But then I have to go and get all male."

". . ."

"When I try to conjure up that female space now – conjure it with my mind, I mean, not just feel it – it's like I'm going to be smothered, suffocate, have to open all the windows, let in the air, speak French, and especially write, write, to open up that space. But the problem is it means that when I'm writing, there's always a cold draught, I'm never comfortable."

Behind the suffocation, or the contrasting fear of penetration and monkeys, some desire is stirring. But even if it shows itself, what difference will it make, when in any case it's all coming to an end?

Fuck it – shout it out in any case:

"What I want now is what I've never had. I want to write from within the warmth of that kitchen, not to be forever whipping myself stravaiging the gale. I want to see the world, outside and in, from the juste distance, as it requires and deserves to be seen."

Can't think what else to say to reveal that glimpse of another life, in which I would be home, and at the same time free to wander – wander in my own words.

He apparently can't either, since – "Eh bien."

I searched for a term with which to describe that presentiment I'd felt of *home*, with its warmth and comfort, as if place and name were one. And I fell back on my old friend, *trust*, to which I attached *confidence*: trust or confidence, at such privileged moments, and not just of Mamet's kind, that there was a place of belonging, as well as a continuity or story which informs and subtends my existence.

My doubts about any solid sense of "association" or "individuation" hadn't disappeared. For this confidence or trust couldn't be summoned at will, it refused to become a means to an end, a straightforward route to any new stability. From the moment I tried to try to grasp my masterplot, seize it in its unity, it shot off in several directions, all of which appeared important, which then bifurcated, trifurcated, intersected, changing names along the way, until my story was more confused and noisy than Spaghetti Junction.

If there were a story subtending and sustaining me, then it could only be *told*. Even if in the telling it would transform and multiply, so completely that, to use a well-worn analogy, it would be like Jason's ship the Argo, which goes through so many storms and has so many of its planks replaced, that by the time it gets back home there's not a single piece the same as what originally set out. (As I thought of this analogy I wondered if I hadn't chosen it for reasons quite other than the obvious one. Because, perhaps, it allowed me to contemplate for a moment the beautifully named *Golden Fleece*; which I then turned into French, the *Toison d'Or*, which made me think not only of Burgundy with its deep, inviting wine cellars, but also of how the word *toison* could be used of a woman's pubic "bush", concealing her "covered way" – and there I was, off again!)

There *was* a story in such moments of confident interiority, but it was a story with no name – certainly not "My Story", nor that of "Dan Gunn". And my sense that it *made sense* was in inverse proportion to my ability to accomplish that making.

Anyone who has reached the end of Proust's great novel is likely to feel that within these volumes is contained an entire world, to which instant access can be gained – there is no other novel which yields such a voluptuous feeling of fullness, in every paragraph and page. Yet when you actually open the novel and start to read, not only do you realise how much you've forgotten, but also that there are passages, and even characters, that you're *glad* to have forgotten; there are so many plots and subplots that you can't possibly keep them all in your head at once; and even a single sentence is beyond the capacity of your breath and brain, it's so packed with parentheses and asides. And so? And so you go back a few pages, then back a few more, or jump forward, trying to find an appropriate place to start re-reading what you had thought was already well absorbed. You try to read more scrupulously this time, knowing that you'll only ever read differently, liking new characters, loathing old favourites, skipping some pages, delighting in others.

The nearer I came to the end of the analysis, the more frequently I received the presentiment of an underlying or overarching story, which would, could I tell it, start to tell me in turn. But when I started to tell it, I found the sentences slipping away from me. I wished all the more keenly that the Sergeant would tell it for me, giving me at last some return on my investment, or putting *his* mouth, as it were, where *my* money had bountifully been.

Despite which pressure I had just enough lucidity left to think: What sort of a room was it in which Proust, famously, wrote the better part of his novel? A *cork-lined* room. Why? Because he needed to keep out the noise, obviously. But also perhaps because he needed to keep *in* his own silence.

The closer I came to the end, the more I urged the Sergeant to talk. Yet the closer I came to the end, the more I hoped he would be silent. For silence, blankness, whiteness, stupidity even, seemed to be the preconditions for that momentary interiority where name and place are one, that confidence which brings the story within reach; even if, in pursuing it, noise quickly interfered again, of cork ripping, of subplots racing round Spaghetti Junction, of Jason hammering a new plank in place, or even of sheep bleating, be they dirty white or golden.

Saturday 16 December
Morning

Dream fragment that I'm in somebody's car, in the passenger seat, and the car is about to skid off the road. Uncontrollable. Jerk awake.

Of all dreams, since starting analysis this has been the most regular visitor. It did happen of course, when I was seventeen, with Matthew driving, on the Isle of Arran. When the car hit ice, it spun, rolled, ended up on the shore – who knows how we all survived. But that hardly explains the recurrence, with the variants involving aeroplanes missing runways, trains going off the rails, and even ships running aground.

Eve always says, when my jerk wakes her up:

"If you haven't got to the bottom of your derailments by now, then maybe there's no bottom. Why don't you just accept that you like to be out of control?"

Afternoon

Cycle to dance class. Fortunately going slow past the Porte St Denis. A mountain-bike flashes past in front of me. Slam on the brakes. Too late, the second bike charges into me. I fly off towards the right.

He must have gone straight through a red light, but I can hardly blame him. I've often done the same these past weeks. But then he gets up and cycles off without so much as checking if my leg is broken or not. Feel like cycling after him and wringing his neck – only I'm still on my back on the asphalt.

Check body: bad contusions and grazes on elbows and knees, but that seems to be the worst of it. Should go back to Justine's and apply ice-packs, but go on to dance class instead. (Did I say "dance class"? Hobble class more like.)

Rubbing the bruises now, hours later. Beckett's remark about how he "fell into the ditch of writing". Can't resist asking: Was last night's dream prophetic? Did I cycle myself into trouble?

Answer: No – even if I did fall "towards the right", "vers le droit", "towards the law". For twelve years I cycled round British towns and never once fell badly. But then British cyclists do not usually go full speed through red lights. A dream can be just a dream, an accident an accident – one which could easily have been worse. Cycling in Paris is dangerous, as I warned the Sergeant when I made up my métro-versus-cycling analogy.

Would the Sergeant have come to my hospital bedside for the final 3 sessions if the accident had been worse? No chance! But

I'd have made it to his place even if on crutches, a parrot on my shoulder for equilibrium.

Evening

Eve asks me to help her put up her pretty Swiss Christmas decorations. I agree, but oh so reluctantly, wondering: Who are they for?

What's more futile than such questions posed of rituals. Emblems of her childlessness, of mine, of ours.

Maybe just upset about the ticket to Scotland. When I tell her I've bought it for her she just shrugs. She tells me, "I suppose you can stay if you want to". But that's no invitation. So despite aching body, get on the bike and leave, feeling dismal.

What does quitting analysis signify about my ability, or as it currently appears inability, to construct a real story with a woman? So much future here, and a torrid past, but no present. Yet.

Try to distract myself by browsing through Justine's bookshelves, and come across a copy of my Psychoanalysis and Fiction. Forgot I gave her a copy all those years back. Makes me queasy, thinking of all I imagined about analysis before I'd so much as set foot inside an analyst's door. Resist dipping into it by ordering myself to get into the bath and soak my bruises.

Your story, look! My story!

But the eyes get raised, and it's gone. All that's left is the shadowy outline of the rules and taboos, as it were the grammar and syntax of the story, which are none the less determining for being hard to define.

"Do you think that rules cannot be analysed?"

My very desire to define the rules of my story was now itself one of the rules, which risked obstructing vision of the rest. It was surely not just transport strikes or building sites or students' papers or sore knees which were preventing me from grasping my story and its plot.

What was it, then?

If I was unable to grasp my own story, then it wasn't just because I couldn't bear the sound of my own voice. It was also because I couldn't hear my own *silence* – my own blankness, whiteness, stupidity. Not just my forgettings, or what analysts would call my "repressions" or "resistance". No, that silence without an apprehension of which any grasp upon a story, a human being, a writer, can only be partial.

As I dodged cars and pedestrians, I thought back to the meeting I'd had six years before, which in its casual way determined so much of what was to follow.

I rabbit on for half an hour with my litany of woes. In response to which, Guy Breton, the psychoanalyst friend to whom I've turned, tells me that from what he can make out, a male analyst might be best for me. And then he says: "You don't need someone who intervenes a lot, someone rather who'll let you talk, who'll let you get on with it yourself."

I stare at him in a mime of intelligent understanding.

"Do-it-yourself as you British say."

He gives me two names and addresses, both men, one of which I instantly discard, since visiting him would mean tripping over the poodles and diplomats in the stiflingly bourgeois suburb of Neuilly-sur-Seine.

And after those two initial meetings with the Sergeant, during the second of which I spoil his drill by telling him that one does not *make* dreams in English, DIY is what it indeed becomes.

There was a dream from some time in the second year which I rediscovered now in these final weeks and revived in the cinema of my head. In it I became a member of the French Resistance, in hiding from the Nazis. To escape capture, I devise the stratagem of diving into a pond and breathing through a snorkel made of a hollow reed shaped like a capital S.

When I recount the dream, it elicits a chortle from the Sergeant.

I try to dot the i's, cross the t's, and unbend the S's: that my "resistance" to analysis is running high (as psychoanalysts like to call the inner fight against the transference), that the Sergeant is a Nazi (unmistakable), that I'd like to hide from him, and that my lifeline (since man is but a "thinking reed") is provided by words. It even occurs to me that words, in Lacan's theory, or "signifiers", are referred to by a capital S, unless it's concepts or "signifieds" (in my somewhat dyslexic way I was always confusing this couple).

The only thing being that, by the time I dot these i's, cross these t's, and confuse these S's, the Sergeant is no longer laughing. Not speaking either, and certainly not admiring how I'm using psychoanalytic terms. Not laughing or speaking or admiring. Just listening.

DIY.

I was always hawklike in my attention to his every rare utterance, but now, four years on from that dream, the hawk was a peregrine, and hungry. By this time I'd almost ceased to hope that my Nazi Sergeant was going to unfurl the bloody red carpet of my Oedipal stage, and I was convinced I had "soiled his chances" (as I put it) with the anal stage by making him jealous of me with Roberta. As for any putative genital stage, my dreams seemed to be informing me that I'd be lucky to get there before my time was up. Yet if full-blown explanations of my stages were too much to hope for, then the odd phrase at least, by way of indication.

Surely!

If not "resistance" or "signifier", then some other textbook terms. Even without recourse to the chicanery of "individuation" or "archetype", there remained a whole cluster of family favourites: "repression", "projection", "introjection", "castration", "fixation". Or how about "aggressivity", "deprivation", "envy", or "acting-out"? Or some of the more arcane terms from Lacan: "Imaginary", "foreclosure", "phallus", or "jouissance"?

I went through the terms in my head, crossing them off the list, confirming that the Sergeant never used them. And then I started on terms less technical or specialised, what I sometimes thought of as the "grand axes" of *my own* analysis: "mourning", "paternity", "crime", "guilt", "farewell" (which motley crew summed up a good deal of the first three years, years of "The Father", in which I tried to grieve him out of my system); "separation", "perversity", "bisexuality", "voice", "farewell" (which covered much of the second triennium, years of "The Son", in which I tried to let go of my mother, pass on from being son, if not to being *father*, then at least to being *adult*).

I used these terms often enough.

But the Sergeant?

"Hmmmm" – if I was lucky. Or "Hmmmm?" Or the faint scratch of his pen across paper, as it – I hoped – took notes.

Impatience turned to disquiet. And the fact that when I ran through the list and summed up my years I in fact produced a travesty, reducing so much that was varied and variegated, so many curses and puns, into pre-packed deep-frozen packets from the Mama-Papa-Pipi-Caca factory, only served to add an edge to this disquiet.

For where *I* could not find, there should *he*. Speak up, surely, and if not with psychoanalytic jargon, nor with my own reductive terminology, then with his own, newly minted. He should astonish me with their gleam, and in that moment pay me back.

Sunday 17 December

Here's not all about Eve, but some about Eve that I like:

> Her slim ankles contrasting with her frighteningly strong thighs
> Her capacity to mimic anyone she meets, capturing them in a couple of gestures
> The speed of her thoughts when they're carried by desire
> Her ability (surely associated) to detect in others their erogenised zones (even when these are as obscure as the elbows or armpits – never known her get it wrong)
> The way she used to read historical romances before I met (and corrupted) her

> Her immobility when standing on pointe
> Her pessimism
> The violence with which she <u>turns</u>
> The fist-strong grip of her innermost muscles.

My tables! Meet it is I set it down that one may smile, be called "Dan Gunn", be a villain, and say "I love you", or more precisely "I <u>do</u> love you".

By her inflated expectation Eve nearly boxed me in, for I've never been good at performing on cue. But I caught her in an unguarded moment this afternoon, as she was concentrated upon her own pleasure. I felt her body change tone, not go limp exactly, but as if the fascia had absorbed honey, becoming softer, more elastic.

Pleased, at first, that she said nothing to acknowledge my unprecedented declaration, just continued inexorably on her way. But later, standing with a cocktail in my hand in the poshest flat I've ever seen in Paris, pretending to be a grown-up and represent the university, wonder: What if she didn't hear me? Maybe my voice let me down and I didn't say it loud enough?

Confirm my suspicion, swaying home to Justine's on my bike, after far too many cocktails and far too much adulthood, by the fact that my declaration made no inroads on her conviction that, since I'm "abandoning" her, she needs to get rid of me first, and so rejects the plane ticket.

"Get out!" she says, "before you get out."

Like a child playing with its scabs, or like myself playing with the grazes on my elbows and knees, I was forever reminding the Sergeant that he could and should speak up. And I had some new ammunition, for during a tramp across Paris I finally asked Christopher about that acquaintance of his who'd been in analysis with my Sergeant for some years.

"Does he ever speak to her?" I ask him.

"You're sure you want to know?" he's delicate enough to reply.

"Better late than never."

"Not only does he speak," Christopher tells me, "but he speaks a lot, a right tea-party they seem to have."

"What!"

Am I delighted or horrified? Delighted at being different? Or horrified that this difference signifies a verdict of no hope?

This was new ammunition all right, yet for some reason I chose not to use it. I kept this information to myself, that with others the Sergeant was voluble. Or, as I thought of it, I stored it along with the other secrets, milk teeth, and "big dreams" under my pillow, hoping the fairies would come and take them in the night, leaving behind a silver sixpence.

Another under-pillow secret: my hope that, where I wasn't getting far with putting my mouth where my money was, I might be achieving it through my writing.

Not that I didn't talk about my writing to the Sergeant, journal excluded. But whereas I was forever going on about his other silences, I never mentioned the fact that he never talked about what I wrote. Is it that I expected him, like any good fairy, to be able to read my thoughts?

Early in 1992, when I'd been seeing the Sergeant scarcely a year, a French translation of my book *Psychoanalysis and Fiction* came out, and I noticed the Sergeant's name on the publisher's list for a free copy. Two sessions later he pointed to a copy of my book on his table and nodded thanks. And that was that – though there was plenty in *my* mind of the "But you say in your book" variety.

Two years later I gave him a copy of *Almost You*, and he thanked me for it, nothing more. When advising me on the sort of analyst he imagined I needed, Guy Breton had added: "He should on no account be tempted to interpret what you write". I was starting to wonder if the Sergeant had spoken to Breton (they were colleagues after all). And, though I kept my perception of his reticence strictly to myself, I was as avid for his comments as I was fearful of them. I wished him to pronounce, pass judgement – favourable of course. And when that didn't happen, I cursed him silently, and then cursed myself.

And I did worse. For now I opened the copy of my book which Justine had on her shelf. I hadn't so much as dipped into it since I started with the Sergeant. But with one week to go I ignored my own better instincts. I skimmed through the chapters and fixed on the conclusion, where I read, with queasiness turning to panic:

> The analyst's desire is given substance, or is embodied, in his or her words, but also in the silence of listening, through which the patient is called upon to speak. For as long as the patient is speaking, the analyst's silence may be seen as required and even commanded by the patient. While the patient is speaking, the analyst's silent attention is the necessary other (or unconscious) which the patient is "racked by" and "in search of" – towards which the patient's words can be said to be "en route". The patient's words thus form a sort of ceaseless commentary on the silence of the analyst.

Yugh!

Why did my heart sink so sickeningly? Of course, I'd got some bits wrong, overstressing the analyst's interpretation, when I could count the Sergeant's interpretations on the fingers of one hand, which is to say less than one a year. And then his silence was not just enjoined by the fact that I was speaking, but also by the fact that I too (until I'd hear the coin drop), was silent, which meant he was also listening to me listening (to him listening, and so on).

But it wasn't what I'd got wrong which upset me. No, what was sickening was just how much I had got *right*. So much of what I'd imagined had come true. The whole course of the six years was suddenly explicable by the simple fact that before I'd even started, the Sergeant had read my book, or during those first two weeks when he was still relatively talkative. He'd decided not to disappoint me, only outdoing my account by the very intensity of his reticence.

I suddenly saw myself in some Edinburgh bar, glancing up to Jimmy the bartender.

Jimmy catches my eye. "The usual, Danny?" he asks. "A pint ay silence?"

In my good moments, as I faced the imminence of the end, I told myself that the fact I'd been able to imagine aspects of analysis such as the predominance of silence was no cause for despair, since I had also acted upon the need to do more than just imagine it. And if my imagination hadn't got it all wrong, then this signalled that analysis did partake of and prolong the processes which concerned the rest of my life – words, bodies, writing, engenderment, sex. A blessed continuity.

But in bad moments I told myself I was a fool for having written that book, a bigger fool for having opened it again at this crucial moment. Even if the Sergeant hadn't read it, I'd done more than just "required and even commanded" his silence. I'd rendered it incontrovertible, I'd *commandeered* it as surely as the Government had the bâteaux-mouches. I'd shoved it down his throat by my incessant babble. And so, rather than encountering any genuine "other" (not to mention the barrackroom lawyer he apparently was with his other patients), I'd only found versions of my boring old self. So it was all just Me Me Me. Just mental masturbation, or a massive con-trick, a great late-twentieth-century version of The Emperor's New Clothes. I'd have been as well just holding on to my imaginings, and I'd certainly have been richer.

I'd never really started at all, and so of course would never end: I'd bullied him into echoing the monotonous drone of a tired old song.

Monday 18 December

Why not just one or t'other? Not analysis alone nor writing alone? Why the compulsion to talk about writing in analysis and about analysis here in this writing? But note the asymmetry, since I haven't breathed a word to the Sergeant about this journal. Not a word to him about my big dreams which might make little dreams.

The strikes are gradually being broken, and I haven't even had time to find out who's won. I'll see out this period on the bicycle, can't bear the idea of gofering down the tunnels. Pedalling like Molloy with one leg if I have to, since the right has seized up with its bruises.

Call in on Edith Brentova to use her computer for another irate letter to the insurance men. First she has to exit from her program of the heavens. Wonder why I've never consulted her, though I know several folk who have successfully. I've about as much confidence in an astrologer telling me the truth about myself as I do a psychoanalyst.

The chart on the screen reminds me of the métro, the Zodiac signs pretty stations. Imagine all those charts, those lives, spinning on the disk inside her computer, and that if I were in there I could seep into all the others in a promiscuous embrace. Ask Edith how she'd guess my chart would look.

"I don't have to guess."

"You mean I'm in here with all the rest."

"You're not, but your chart is."

"Nice idea. What's it look like?"

"I thought it would be very organised and regular, but it turns out to be just the opposite, chaotic."

Glad for that, though I don't ask to know more.

No word yet from Eve about the ticket. She is going to spend Christmas by herself, I know it. Justine tells me I should thrust the ticket upon her.

Thoughts of how the Sergeant laughed 6 years ago when I managed to dupe him into lowering the price and then started coming three times a week. Still hoping that a story may emerge for what I want to write next, and that it will, when he reads it, elicit another such a laugh. Stare hard at the panel of my unfinished triptych, and what do I see?

What I glimpse there is a blank, an absence, or maybe a refutation: No, you did not kill your father, though you will have to relearn this every day of your life. No, were you ever to leave home, this would be no betrayal or crime, just the way of the world, as the trees bend and the tides ebb and flow, generation after generation.

Stare harder, and as I do so, shout: "But I <u>want</u> <u>to</u> commit a crime! And a big one! For and against the Sergeant!"

Then see my shout – yes <u>see</u> it – carried down the glen. And if I continue to stare hard – yes, <u>stare</u> – what's that I see, echoing off the rocks? I could almost swear it's not my voice now, nor any human noise, but the sound, so hopeful, of bleating.

Maybe it was the second of the alternative readings of the Sergeant's silence, the one from the bad moments, that helped me appreciate the jokes and jibes both Eve and Justine would make about my analyst and analysis. For me, these jokes testified to just how odd they judged my persistence to be.

"Can't believe you're still going."

"Your man still as chatty?"

"Still droning out the monologue?"

"Now you're ending, you can try it out by yourself – given he says nothing you might not notice the difference."

If I enjoyed such remarks, it was because they reminded me that whatever I'd been able to imagine years before, the reality was surely stranger – weird, grotesque, intriguing.

We all have mixed feelings about encounters with those in the "caring professions", and about what we get told, or not told, by them. Anyone who has experienced a therapy, be it psychic, physical, or psychosomatic, has experienced something of my two alternative readings of silence. Anyone who consults a doctor over a period of time, still more a so-called "specialist" or "consultant", lives a double-edged ending.

My ambivalence was directed at the little ending, closure, or death, that occurs every time a demand is being made of someone in authority – and there's a demand whenever there's payment, suffering, or both. Even if the analyst, therapist, counsellor, or consultant, has the decency to pronounce in clear terms a verdict or diagnosis, there's likely to remain a question in the mind of the patient, a question directed at a silent core or heart within the pronouncement. It's here that different versions of my ending are to be found, versions which can go from the not-quite-reassuring to the downright terrifying.

At times it can be as simple as the following: The Authority – doctor, analyst, specialist, whoever – isn't telling you much because in fact there's nothing wrong with you and so nothing to report. This is the benign version. But it will be rubbing shoulders with an aggressive neighbour. This neighbour grates: Authority isn't telling you much, on the contrary, because there's something *horribly* wrong.

The problem doesn't stop here. For Authority may show signs of being sympathetic. He (who can on occasion be She) may deign to stop at the foot of your bed or couch and smile to you or exchange a greeting. He's taking your feelings into account. Yet this kindness can very quickly become a new sort of cruelty if it indicates that the objectivity of His judgement is becoming clouded. This can give: Authority's telling you a lot about your condition, maybe too much – in fact He may even be embellishing. And He's doing so because He's sure that the more you hear the more you'll be reassured. As if that weren't bad enough, this cruel suspicion also has a raucous neighbour, sharing the very same corner of silence at the heart of Authority. The neighbour goes: Authority is telling you a lot, may even be embellishing, yet He's still not telling you the whole story. He's not telling you all because He sees the susceptible sort of person you are, and believes you're not up to hearing, still less handling, the whole truth.

Any way it comes, it's the patient, the person making the demand, who is in the precarious position. While what my jousts with the Sergeant's silence told me is that, the less specific or nameable the thing being demanded, or the less specific the hurt or symptom, the more intense that precariousness may become.

"You've read Franz Kafka, haven't you?" Justine would tease me, when I raised the matter with her.

And it's true, a lot of it should have been obvious from Kafka, whose work offers as good a training for contact with medical authorities as any that exists. There can never be a true *dialogue* between yourself (a poor mortal, a patient, an unexceptional human creature) and Authority. The extra twist being that, the more urgent the demand upon your analyst, doctor, dentist, specialist, the more He becomes invested with Authority (capital A). In such a *non-dialogue* between patient and Authority, the patient goes through periods of self-accusation for not having properly explained the situation – not having found the precise words to describe the symptom; and other periods in which the patient accuses Authority of being stone deaf and incapable of understanding the perfectly adequate description just given.

And as Kafka warns us, things can always get worse.

For you can be feeling so damned awful that you know you're going to die. It may be just a fear, of course, but then there's absolutely no difference at this moment between a certainty and a fear, unless the other, Authority, can teach you that difference. That is the job of Authority, a job which requires getting rid of that core of silence once and for all.

Yet at this very moment it's silence making itself heard again, giving the nightmare that: Authority is keeping quiet, not telling you the truth, and you're surely destined to die, because it's clear He doesn't know a damned thing about you. And this nightmare also has a neighbour, there exists a final turn of the screw where silence is concerned: Authority is keeping quiet, not telling you the truth, because He *does* know, He knows it all – the Bastard knows that you're almost dead already.

One little word speaks to this silence which I heard behind the fascination at my persistence with the Sergeant, and which most patients auscultate in dealings with doctors or therapists.

It catches both sides of the hope and fear, the scant reassurance *and* its noisy aggressive neighbour. When it occurred to me, I figured it was such a common word that we all have access to it. But then I tried pronouncing it within the analysis, immediately translating it, and then realised that it's one of the precious gifts of the English language.

The word is: *over*.

And I went through a few of the word's cognates – "over it", "get over it", "it's over"; as against "left-over", "left over", "all over" – so as to convince my own Authority, my Sergeant, of what the French are missing.

Tuesday 19 December
Morning

Wake with a sore throat, mouth, gums – some bit of me is paying for the words of love I spoke to Eve. And still she hasn't told me for Scotland. Maybe she'll phone today?

The first métros must be running, since I see pedestrians dive into stations. Not I. I'll buy a helmet when I have the time, armour-plating if needs be.

Exams all marked, final conversations with the lawyers today. Closing things off – not taps, they've been closed for months – in preparation for departure. Buy Justine a Christmas hamper to thank her for the use of her flat. Haven't even begun to think of Italy yet, though did just manage to find a flat to rent in Bologna. Anyway, no need to start worrying about Italy now, that future will be different from anything I can presently imagine – though how, I cannot, of course, imagine.

Evening

Twenty-five minutes the Sergeant keeps me waiting, as I curse the métros that have made the traffic lighter, encouraged the faint-hearted to start coming again. (I imagine his patients, the ones with whom he converses, to be well-heeled self-indulgent obese spoiled neurotic members of the haute bourgeoisie, all driving luxury cars, wearing Givenchy, smoking expensive cigarettes which befoul the waiting room, wiping foie-gras from their fingers as they prepare to shake the Sergeant's hand.)

On the couch: droning on about how he's failed to give me even the slightest indication of whether or not I'm right to end now. Expand into an indictment of how he's never given me the slightest indication of whether I'm at least on the right path, whether I'm on a path at all — I admit there could be several right paths. Tell him I could be thick in the forest, or up shit creek, or about to step into an animal trap, and he wouldn't even raise his voice to warn me. Not once has he tried to redirect me even slightly.

"Am I to suppose," I ask him, "that this is because I've been perennially on course? Or because you haven't the slightest clue what the course should be? Or that you actually enjoy watching me wade up the creek through the shit? Or you simply can't be bothered taking your nose out of whatever treatise you're writing — in which I suppose you do use some of your profession's preferred jargon — or the women's magazines or the Harlequin romances?"

". . ."

"For all I know you've got a tiny video machine back there, and you're busy jerking off on pornographic films!"

Remain lucid enough to admit to myself that these accusations have an autobiographical ring to them — it's doubtless how I would spend my time if I were forced to listen to the daily ritournelles of the foie-gras guzzlers.

All the time, pulsing in the background, the fact that time is short — shorter — shortest.

Let me pin him down: "You know there's one thing you can't pretend not to want to speak about: if I'm really finished here. Or just interrupting. I'll explain to you."

Do I really hear him sigh, or is that my paranoia?

"Of course, I'd like you to indicate that this is a real ending, more than just an interruption. That even if I have gone up a few shit creeks, I've got there in the end. Yes, I could go on producing dreams and thoughts and desires, until one of us gives out. But something's been accomplished, enough to call it a day. There's hope for me in that, since I can go on by myself, or maybe in company with another living human being."

"Really?"

"But you know that if you do that, tell me I'm over the worst, then you close the door, slam it and lock it behind me, there's no route back, and I'm out there in the cold. And you know who did that to me?"

". . ."

"The father, maybe all fathers do that to their sons, but mine did it especially when he closed the door and died."

". . ."

"And then of course I'd like you to tell me that, though something's been achieved, some distance travelled, there's still a way to go, words to open new vistas and let me become a much freer person than I am today. There's hope in that future too, since I still feel so half-baked, and it means at least I can be sure of returning."

". . ."

"But if you tell me it's not over, or even just intimate that it may not be over, then you're leaving the door wide open. Then all the air — my air — is being sucked back in here, I might as well not even attempt to leave, you'll always be here waiting. And you know who did that to me?"

I suppose he can guess, so I don't bother waiting. "The mother, my mother, maybe all mothers do it to their sons, and we boys are forever trying to say farewell to her."

". . ."

"Those are 2 futures, but at least they're futures. Come on!

Saying nothing is no future at all." Pause to let that sink in. "I've got 2 sessions left, and I feel I've barely started."

"Eh bien."

⬦

If the word "over" was on my lips during the final weeks, then it was surely because, whether in its more reassuring or more worrying aspect – if these can ever be fully separated – it was never on the lips of the Sergeant.

I goaded, insulted, challenged him to pronounce, take a risk, a risk to which I claimed I would respond, coming forth to meet him on some middle ground. Though even as I did so I wondered if his very silence wasn't the biggest risk of all, a risk which would have been spoiled had he once, just once, tried to explain or justify this silence, but which he did not – silent even, or especially, about his own silence.

Or at least, I *say* he was silent.

But was he?

When I read through the conclusion to my *Psychoanalysis and Fiction* I was perturbed by how many elements of the experience I had "pre-imagined". Yet there was something, not an element this time, something larger, which I had pre-imagined all wrong, and which promised to falsify the rest. While cycling round the streets one day I saw it, or rather heard it: the *tone*. The tone of my book when speaking of analysis was pious, hushed, almost sacral. The silence I invoked gave back echoes of vestal chambers, resonant halls, respectful distances, the analyst drawing the patient forward like a priest or a shaman.

In all my genuflecting and swinging of censers, I forgot to pre-imagine that this silence might also throb with: the noise of cars accelerating down the quai, the pre-recorded voice in Japanese explaining the sights to tourists on the bâteaux-mouches, the honking of a thousand horns during the strikes, the light tread of the analyst's wife as she goes in and out of her adjacent room, the telephone ringing, the buzzer announcing the next patient (who would sometimes arrive before I uttered a single word), the analyst's breathing, his puffing on his cigarette, his fiddling with his papers, toppling a pile of them, a heavy tome sent crashing to the floor.

And I talk of silence! I might as well have been at Hampden, when the roar goes up, or in Milan train station at midday, as I once suggested to him.

And that hubbub wasn't all, since there were two other features which added to the din, kicking on the head of the ideal silence I'd once imagined.

"Hmmmm."

"Hmmmm?"

"Ehmmm."

"Ahh!"

"Ohh!"

"Pffff."

Yes, the lesser of these noisy features consisted in the Sergeant's little noises: "para-lexical elements", they might be called by speech-analysts. I could indeed be forgiven for having thought myself at a football match, the number of senseless noises he managed to emit; or at a psychoanalytic version of Old MacDonald's Farm ("With an oink oink here and an oink oink there"). He wouldn't say, "Would you care to elaborate on that?" or "Very interesting!" He'd say – when "say" is much too dignified – "Hmmmm!" or "Hmmmm?" or "Pffff".

And there was an additional reason why his noises were getting more irritating than ever in the final weeks: because they were so damned hard to *transcribe*. I scratched and fiddled in my journal with all sorts of combinations of letters, but only to come up with some expletive like "Pshaw!" or "Egads!", which placed him not only in the wrong language (since his murmurings were on the fringes of French more than of English) but also in the wrong century. Or then he'd clear his throat deliberately – I was pretty sure I could distinguish the voluntary from the smoker's spasm – and in what language was that, and how was I supposed to write it down?

To my rude assemblages of vowels and consonants, with which I endeavoured to transmit his noises, I added signs such as ". . .", with which I gestured to his worldlessness. *Ellipsis*, the dictionary told me, is where one or more words in a sentence have been omitted or removed which would be required to complete the grammatical construction or fully express the sense. "Cat's got your tongue?" I would occasionally snap at him. His silence was *rapt*. Which is to say, in the context, not so much trancelike as seized, *stolen*.

From whom had the words been stolen? From him? What did I care about that. All I cared was that they'd been stolen from me. They were my due, had been seized before they reached me, and now I might never get them back.

Yes, it was time to do some stealing in turn – to steal from the Sergeant, of course. I wanted something to put in place of his ellipses; or, if that were to prove impossible, at least to *give a place* to what had been stolen. Much as I liked the Bram van Velde and the Bacon, they didn't seem very practicable, and in any case where would I have hung them in my ruin? No, it was another theft of which I was dreaming, a bigger *rapt* I was beginning to conceive.

Tuesday 19 December
(contd, late-night)

"And you won't accept my offer of the ticket?"

"You're clearing out. So go on, get out."

Too tired to argue. Not too tired to shed a quiet tear.

There were *two* features gumming up the ideal analytic silence I'd once pre-imagined. Grunts and sniffs were bad enough; but there was worse. It was an animal impersonation as well, and one equally hard to transcribe. Like rats scuttling, or a hamster gnawing at its cage.

His pen, its writing.

I often supposed (out loud) that he was writing his love letters, his shopping lists, or the script for his new porn movie in which his wife would star.

And then, when my self-esteem was higher, I'd suggest he was writing about me.

Yet if he was writing about me, then he certainly didn't make use of the notes. He never came out and said anything like, "Yes, but back in 1993, as I can see, you mentioned that all-important potty"; or, "My notes suggest that you use that same word, *pipi*, in English and in French". And if he never used his notes, then why was he taking them? For himself? But I knew he had no time to peruse them either after I left or before I entered, since his patients were ever hard on each other's heels. I could only conclude he was taking notes because at some later date he intended to *give me away*.

Not that I minded. On the contrary, as I've said, the fantasy of notoriety appealed to me enormously: I'd become more famous than Freud's Dora or Rat-Man. I thought up titles for his book (or chapter, more modestly): "The Case of the Man who could not French-Kiss"; or "The Sheep-Man: A Case of Animal Identification"; or "The Auld Alliance: A Case of Franco-Scottish Schizophrenia"; or "The Long Goodbye: The Case of the Man who could not say 'Farewell'".

Sure, let him give me away – only let him give me away *once and for all*.

Behind the fantasy of notoriety a fear showed its head.

I imagined how I'd be walking down the rue des Écoles some day in late 1996, after returning from my sabbatical in Italy. I glance into a bookshop window, and there I see the Sergeant's book. I enter the shop, open the book, and I find myself described there in terms – Argh! – which not only are not my own, but which falsify everything, not giving me away at all.

I look for my name and find only "Mr G.", or worse, "Monsieur G.". I search for what I said, find a good deal of it reported more or less accurately. But then I look for what *he* said, or rather puffed, guffawed, and omitted. And in its place, instead of those ellipses, I find not something he stole from me, but, precisely, something he *did not steal*. I find psychoanalytic wisdom. So he's masquerading as a thief, while in fact he's only a pedlar of other folk's wares.

This starts with the surgical gloves of my name, of course, or my lack of it: "Monsieur G.". I paid him so as to be permitted to use his name, if I so chose, his so-called "proper name". He received my money so as to preclude his right to reciprocate (to become like Montgomery Clift in Hitchcock's film *I Confess*). And the travesty doesn't stop here. For it is furthered by the massive transmutation of his own noise and silence.

Transmutation into what?

This was the crucial betrayal that I was determined to stop. It chilled my blood when I imagined reading his book. For transmute it all he would, including me, him, and the whole damned process.

Into what?

Into something serious: something *deadly serious*.

Wednesday 20 December

Heavy sleet but I can't bear to take the métro. Put spare trousers inside a plastic bag in the pannier, and when I get there nip out of the Sergeant's waiting-cubicle to the toilet, change sodden trousers for dry. No point in putting wet shoes back on, so walk into his room in stocking soles, shoes in hand. Soon be down to my underwear at this rate.

Start straight in on the dream, though wondering as I do so if this is really the best way to use up the precious remaining minutes of this penultimate session: "So I'm in your waiting room, which has become the entrance to a zoo, along with many other children, animal noises all round. Hah!"

Shake my head on his bolster: can't believe I'm supposed to be stopping in 2 days' time and I'm producing a dream like this. Jesus! There's enough here for 10 years or more.

"Ehegm?"

"I want to go into the zoo, thinking I can get a kitten for Eve – predictable baby substitute – and there's a strong odour of lions. Not loins, lions – maybe lions' loins. My mother, who's turned up, goes down and steals one of these lion cubs, but when she holds it in her hand it looks like a peeled prawn."

"Hmmmm?"

"The little prawn is like an infant's tiny widdler, that's clear enough, but there's something more."

". . ."

"Prawn, crevette, the little toasts I was served at that posh cocktail party the other night. Canapé! Prawn canapé! Prawn couch, prawn on the couch, your couch, you're ready to sell me into captivity."

Listen closely: he's writing.

"As we leave the zoo my mother complains – she never complains – of an injury to her foot, sustained when visiting the lion house. She asks me to <u>dress</u> the wound, and I see I'll have to fill the hole on the top of her foot with a plug – but what sort of a plug? An ear-plug of course!"

Think about plugs to stop <u>fuites</u>, and the foam kind I sometimes put in my ears so as to sleep at night. When I have them in and then speak, my voice is loud for once, just like he pointed out to me in the very first session.

"Take the plugs from my ears, so I can hear, and then dress and heal my mother. Yes, the kind of plugs you've probably been putting in your ears ever since I started coming here."

"HMMMM!" (He enjoys that.)

"But when the plug starts to expand, I become more and more anxious – can you blame me? I'm worried my mother's wound really will heal."

"And the plug will get sumuck?"

"Sorry?" I'll never get his wavelength.

"'And the plug will get stuck?'"

"And then start to rot, even though as I look at it I see it's turned transparent — transparent again, like that transparent member of mine."

How to describe the fact that I'm both intensely anxious and thoroughly amused by the recounting of this dream, the strangest cocktail — cock-tail!

Hear him scribbling away.

"Have you got the title right?" I ask him. "The film about the lion-cub I'd like to be in, it's called Born Free. Born, not Reborn, enough of the Renatos."

"Ahhh!"

"But a question, mine: How do I get free, of you, of him, whoever him is, of her, my mother, of my past? Comment me débarasser de tout?"

"Partir?"

"Was that a question?"

". . ."

"Leave", he said, "partir". But did I hear him right? Plugs out!

"But how do I leave you, leave them, in such a way that I don't annihilate you all? Wish to acknowledge all they've done, all you've done for me, the fact that my mother never made unreasonable demands. I want to leave you all. Thank you, then leave you."

"Eh bien!" He's suddenly on his feet.

Pay him the 250 francs I've remembered to transfer from the wet trousers to the dry. He surprises me now.

"About Friday," he starts.

"Yes?"

"I was wondering if we could make it Thursday, tomorrow?"

"Make Friday Thursday — why not?

"Midday, then?"

I note it in my diary, then walk out, neglecting to look at my watch.

Get soaked again in the sleet, and stay soaked this time, getting colder by the minute as I cycle round the city on what I hope will be final errands: bank, lawyer, builder, responsibility now in their hands. Take hamper to Justine, balancing it on handlebars. I'm out of here in 4 days' time and hope not to be back for 9 months.

Wondering: Why did the Sergeant change the day for the final session, when he's never changed a session since I started, even in normal times? Why does this not fill me with panic? Why am I happy at the sudden bending of the rules?

I realised at last what it was so bothered me about the ending of David Mamet's film *House of Games*: the con-man doesn't deserve to die.

The obsessive psychiatrist finally twigs, though more by chance than by deduction, that she's been set up from the start. She makes her way to the bar where her one hundred and eighty thousand dollars are being divided up amongst the con-men on the team. She learns that Joe Mantegna, the boss, will be taking a flight to Las Vegas that evening. She intercepts him at the airport, leads him off to a hangar, then fills him full of bullets. Maybe this is part of his con-trick, and the psychiatrist's gun is loaded with blanks, but I don't think so. The film, alas, does turn *serious*. Perhaps the psychiatrist did need to commit a crime; but not this one, not one which has anything tragic to it.

She should have seen the funny side, but she doesn't. And in the end Mamet doesn't either, and so he goes for an ending which seems violent but in fact is much less violent than it would have been had the psychiatrist found some comic way out of the theatricality, back into reality.

All that silence and all that noise. What was it I feared the Sergeant would do with all that silence and all that noise, in these final sessions, or afterwards in his writing which I imagined emerging from our encounter? I thought again of the hushed tone of my *Psychoanalysis and Fiction*. I feared lest he turn them into something similar, even worse something didactic, worse still something tragic, justifying his tone by the fact that so much of the six years had been taken up with pain and loss and grief.

Not that I wished to deny the pain or loss or grief. I myself had done a quantity of writing where these had been prominent. What is more, the years of analysis had not only been *about* these, but had enjoined them too, and I had found myself losing intimates, ambitions, plans, certainties, old and familiar maladies, and as I've said the major part of my brain. I believed that my life would continue to be led under the sign of a premature death, my father's, as if it were my Zodiac, and that I'd forever be returning to that sign, that source, to read, reread, interpret it anew.

No, I didn't wish to deny, or to have the Sergeant deny, the pain, the loss, or the grief. Yet if these were to prevail, and cloud the noisy silence of which he had offered me an abundance, then I should indeed feel betrayed.

But if I was right in thinking that it was not a tragic tale which needed to be told, then what was it?

When I tried to imagine how I could commit a crime against the Sergeant, and when stealing his paintings seemed implausible, I only briefly imagined cornering him, as in Mamet's film, and gunning him down. For that too would be overly devotional and pious. When what I needed was a crime which truly corresponded to our years together (though "together" was a misnomer), to their silence and noise, and to all that these elided. A crime, but not tragic; a theft, but not material; a betrayal, but not serious. For – and this, I thought, would be the very hardest thing to describe – the years of noise and silence, despite the pain and loss and grief, had not been tragic or serious, or not that alone, since they had also been . . .

What?

They had also been hilarious. They had been one long hugely protracted *joke*!

This was truly scandalous – so scandalous that I almost fell off my bicycle when I admitted it to myself. There's nothing inherently scandalous about tragedy or loss. But a con-trick? A joke?

If it was a joke, then it was one to which he would never be able to give the punch-line, in his all-too-ponderous writing with its professional strictures and its need to exemplify. But it would, if told correctly, give us both away, in our individual and shared absurdity.

Not once, not even when I was getting up from his couch with my head in bloodied bandages and was longing for a man to hug, not once, though I knew that by asserting it I was invoking every demon from the depths (or shallows) – not once did the joke become inaudible. It was indeed a crime: as the saying goes, it was a *bleeding crime*.

"Wipe that smile off your face, boy!"

When my first primary-school teacher, Miss Ogilvie, wasn't ordering me to "Buck up!" in class, or tweaking my ear, she was usually shouting this at me: to ignore or forget the joke. It was one thing the Sergeant never told me: neither in his words (never bringing it all back to him), nor in his silence or his noise. When I thought of them now, all his elisions, even when I confronted them in their fell forking form – He's keeping quiet because he *doesn't* know; Keeping quiet because he *does* know – their whiteness seemed like a chuckle. Like my own chuckle which he was stealing from me. Like that chuckle he let out, followed by a long laugh, when I'd stolen from him six years before, duping him into giving me three sessions a week at a discount rate.

The silence was chuckling, though the punch-line was lacking. Its whiteness was drawing me on, it had a warmth to it – not a human warmth, nothing to do with "empathy" or "sharing"; more like an animal warmth, and it felt to me somewhat soft, somewhat fleecy. Foolish, certainly, but glad of such folly, even in its darkest moments.

I stared again at the blank central panel on my *Ovine Triptych*, and I wondered, as in the jokes of childhood: What is white, fleecy-warm, foolishly contented, and worthy, for me, of a chuckle?

Faith? Was that it?

Or —?

I had one more session in which to find out. But already I could hear the hooves in the distance. And though the films of old told me cavalry, come to save me at the last, when I listened harder, it wasn't horses I was hearing nor soldiers I was glimpsing.

Thursday 21 December

9.30 a.m. Winter solstice. The sun will never rise. Heavy clouds threatening snow. Not a word from Eve.

And here's me hoping for some sweet and simple dream which will speak of resolution, inclusion, reconciliation, even some integration.

Why did the Sergeant change the day? If he hadn't, I'd have had the whole of today to look forward to and prepare for tomorrow. I could have thought over last night's dream. I could have another one tonight, more appropriate.

What do I know. Pack pannier with spare trousers, put on waterproofs, get on the bike.

For once, in the waiting room, wishing he'd take his time. Into the toilet to change my trousers — a disappointing drizzle outside, no snow. Take off my shoes. Strong urge to stride naked into his consulting room. "You see?" I'd shout. "You see?" Though I've no idea what he'd be required to look at. Cursing that dream, which I can't push aside. It promises to eat up all my remaining time, leaving him nothing for the grand summing-up.

Unless maybe he's allotted extra time for this final session?

Conviction that he's not prepared me right. Wonder: Has he let me prepare myself?

His rituals just the same as ever as he draws back the curtain and walks to his armchair. On my back on the couch, thinking about the word he used, "Partir". Then on with the dream, which, from the moment I open my mouth, though it seems convoluted and confused, presents me with three big stages in my life: the present, early adulthood, and then childhood – very convenient.

"So I'm in love with a beautiful black woman called Souang. Madly, hopelessly in love. And she invites me to her village which is also called Souang. There are strikes on, but I decide to try the train, though when I get onto it I've no ticket and in any case it's not about to move. I'll have to get there under my own steam, no public transport."

". . ."

"It's beautiful the way that name and place are one and the same, and I so badly want to reach such a homeland. Then there's Souang's childlike body with her full womanly breasts. And there's something wonderful too in the fact that I can think of no associations to her name. It conjures up nothing but herself and her home, they're identical. Her black skin the perfect opposite and complement to my whiteness and blankness."

Every word I speak, I'm aware not only of what I'm saying but also of the fact that I'm trampling over the few minutes left to me, I'm neither speaking what I have to, nor stopping so as to be fully aware of the time slipping by.

"Part Two, I'm back as I was aged 18, visiting my oldest friend, Matthew. He shows me where, in his basement, there's a concert being rehearsed by the rock group, Queen."

"Chhmm?"

Wonder if he's ever heard of Queen? Can't stand the group myself. Pah! What do I know. For all I know he's out raving every night, dressed in leather chaps, dropping E's.

"Heard yesterday that 'Queen's' is a gay club on the Champs-Elysées."

"Hmmmm!" (He does seem to know about it – maybe he is a raver.)

"They're rehearsing a song called 'We are the Champions'. But it's a farce, since the house they're in is a ruin, and they're bisexual so they can never win, let alone be champions. And I'm so grateful to them for this impossibility, for their farce, for the fact that they don't give a shit about winning or losing."

". . ."

"Matthew shows me a road being cut through the Sussex Downs from near his ruined house to a university, connecting bisexual basement to head. But I must be off, no time even to explain why I'm so in love with Souang and her blackness."

And oh, the need to stop, unpack this — Christ, even a drowning man, between gulps, surely has seconds to linger on some of the highlights. Basements, ruins, Downs, queens, and still the opacity of Souang luring me on — there's enough here for months. If I've been linked to Matthew since we were 5 years old then I'm right, it is surely because that's how old he was when he decided he was bisexual.

"Chgggm." (The Sergeant clears his untranscribable throat.)

"Part Three, and I'm getting off my bike, still en route to SOUANG — see it in capital letters now, like on a road sign. My shoes sink into the melting tar, fixed, fixated, can't go back can't go on, feet getting heavier by the second, jump onto my bicycle just in time before I get stuck for good. Arrive at a schoolhouse, like those of my childhood, where SOUANG is waiting for me. She tells me that in 2 hours she must leave for India."

"India?"

"She's much too dark to be Indian, she's — she's a — <u>tar</u> <u>baby</u>. But all my childhood associations of exotic foreigners are of Indians and Pakistanis, working as grocers in Edinburgh. SOUANG with her place name. She's completely foreign and completely at home. And her black skin is pulling my white towards her. Why, I'm as white as a —"

Break off, for I suddenly know that if I try and say "sheet", I'll say something else, and it's not time yet, no not time yet for that near-rhyme.

"I kiss and caress her in the schoolhouse, undress her, and then am magically naked too. It'll be white on black now or black on white — and yes, it's true, I do always write with a black pen. I'm

155

just about to enter her, she lies so enticingly on her back across the school desk with her legs apart. When in walks a man with no face."

"Hmmmm."

"So my father with no face. But here's the strange bit. I give SOUANG up to him. I'm so glad to do so. He's no rival. I <u>welcome</u> him. Then, just as he's on the point of penetrating her, I wake up. I'm feeling so excited, enthusiastic, my pleasure's not been diminished, it's been increased ten-fold by his presence."

I can't believe I'm coming to the end. Time slipping by me. Panic panic. I can't finish with that.

"But this can't be the last dream-scene I'm going to give you. It's one where I take pleasure by proxy, one which virtually excludes me. I've gone back, but I find myself excluded."

"Really?" He sounds sceptical.

"It gives me nothing at all, unless the excitement, unless –"

It occurs to me, with a start, then a surge of relief – "Unless this account I'm giving you of it, here on this couch."

"Ahh! Indeed! En effet!"

"Little dreams of big dreams? Talk about it, write about it, black on white?"

"Chmmmm!" No question this, but his most positive affirmation.

"I can see that SOUANG – the dark continent – is also woman, women, my mother no doubt. I can see that the man without a face is my father, all men. But – but it's their affair. Let me leave them to it."

"Yes."

And I assert it now as if my life depended on it, the words tumbling out of me:

"Fuck the lot of them, I'm off! Assez de mon père, assez de ma mère! Basta papà, basta mamma! Enough of the father, enough of the mother!"

"Bien!"

Just like that?

It's over, and he's up on his feet.

Wheel my legs over the edge of the couch, stand up, walk forward, put my wet shoes back on, take the 250 francs from my pocket. But he has not advanced as he normally does, towards the door. He's just standing there looking relaxed, smiling, his jacket unbuttoned — that's rare.

"So when are you leaving?" he asks me.

"In three days' time, for Scotland, then on to Italy."

"And you come back to Paris?"

"In September."

He nods, smiling still as if he were highly amused, and I find myself smiling too. He comes towards me, hand outstretched. I give him the money, then I shake his hand, overcoming a momentary urge to embrace him.

"So. Eh bien —"

I face him squarely, not helping him in the least, not turning towards the door as I usually do, just smiling back, giving him the chance to speak.

He raises his eyebrows as if to lob the ball back to me and ask if I have anything to add. But I make it clear from my own smile that now it's *his* turn, his chance, his route to perdition.

His lungs fill. He seems to formulate a momentous thought. He waits for what is an incalculably long time, but may only be seconds. Then, at last, it's out:

"Eh bien — goodbye. Au revoir."

I can't repress a laugh. "Au revoir," I get out in return.

I open the door, the second door, and I leave him to close it behind me, walk briskly down the stairs, not looking at my watch, and not back at the door either.

Only when at the foot of the stair do I recall what it was I meant to tell him, in a formula of hope whose sense is only now becoming clear to me. An expression borrowed, I believe, from the rustlers of the Border-country.

I meant to tell him:

"If I'm going to become a thief, commit a crime, and if I'm going to be hanged for it as I hope, then I may as well be hanged for a sheep as for a lamb!"

The first thing I did when I arrived in Bologna for my sabbatical, after I unpacked, was to write to Eve. I thanked her for coming with me to Scotland, and for the walks we took across the snow-clad hills, the firesides by which we lay together, the hour we spent in front of John Singer Sargent's portrait of Lady Agnew of Lochnaw. I reminded her of some of the fine sheep we'd met, and of the new words we had shared.

The next thing I did was to faint.

One moment I was pacing round the vast airy rooms of the flat which was to be my home for the next nine months, admiring the view, the next I was on my backside on the floor, spasms flowing over and through my sacrum, up into my spine and extremities, from the force of collision.

When I came to my senses I dragged myself onto a chair from which I could see over the terracotta rooftops towards the medieval twin-towers.

Was I still myself? Still "Dan Gunn"? Still the same person I had been these past six years, during which I had lived through an analysis?

Not exactly. But who I was remained to be discovered, or invented.

I was suddenly impatient to start, so there and then I took out the book of unlined A4 paper which I'd bought from my favourite paper shop, Papier Plus, just before I left Paris. And into this I started to write, beginning by transcribing the diary I kept during the last month of the analysis, with respect to which my first-ever fainting fit seemed to offer a brutal somatic caesura. Here, yes here, I realised with a start, staring me in the face, was the blank central panel of my *Ovine Triptych*, waiting to be brought to completion.

Despite my aching backside, I managed to get a few pages down that first day. At the end of which, browsing through the Sunday newspapers I'd picked up on the plane, which were full of reports of the "Lottery Fever" that had beset the British Isles, I realised it was time.

So I set to, and calculated the grand total, until then avoided. I'd been going for five years and eleven months. If I subtracted two months each year for holidays, that made fifty-nine months. At a rate of two hundred and fifty francs a session, seven hundred and fifty a week, three thousand francs a month, the grand total came to – I still could not believe it: a grand total of one hundred and seventy-seven thousand francs. Tax free! At the present rate of exchange, that made twenty-four thousand, two hundred and forty-six pounds, or thirty-two thousand, one hundred and eighty-one dollars. Or – the calculator was about to go on strike – fifty-eight million four hundred and ten thousand Italian lire!

I knew I shouldn't, that it was quite impermissible, that John Knox was preparing to leap out of his grave and strike me down. I knew I shouldn't, but when I thought of all the hours I'd worked to make that money, the years I'd studied, and when I thought what else I could have done with even just a half of it – when I saw the figures, though I knew I shouldn't, I burst out and laughed. I had to be insane.

Fleeced. I'd been *fleeced*!

But in my new life I'd not mind. No, for I'd be sending my analyst a package before long. And when he opened it, after perusing a few Polaroids of Eve and me together, he'd find a wool-covered deluxe boxed set of *The Ovine Triptych*, along with a royalty slip for some obscenely inflated sum, way in excess of one hundred and seventy-seven thousand francs – "For moneys received for *Wool-Gathering or How I Ended Analysis*". On the left margin of this royalty slip he'd see my drawing of a Scotsman in a kilt, and to make sure he got the point, a bunch of thrift in his hand. On the bottom, a doodle of an Irish policeman with the name "Gilhaney" next to it. While on the right, fleecy, white, and foolishly contented, the no-longer "almost you" – the now fully fleeced ewe I have become.

(After reading the book, he goes back to the Polaroids. "Hmm", he thinks, "Eve and Ewe.")

There was just one element I needed to find, and quickly, to get on with it, as I couldn't go on calling my analyst "ZZZZ" for much longer. If I was beginning to reconcoct myself, turning the conditional tense into the present, then I could hardly leave him out of the fun.

The sun is dipping over the rooftops. I drag myself from the chair, and step into the late-afternoon light which is streaming down the elegant porticoes of Strada Maggiore. Of course I have the right to call my analyst by his real name, and I've even started to write about how pseudonyms and abbreviations create an illusion that behind them there lurks the truth, linked to proper names and personal identities. But if withholding his name is going to be misleading, then giving it will be self-defeating. It will narrow the person I know – know so little yet so intensely – to a public figure, one who teaches, writes articles, and appears in the phone book. And any claim I make is somehow bound to have the opposite effect from what's intended.

Musing upon this conundrum, rubbing my bruised buttocks, I stop under the porticoes and stare vacantly into the window of a shop selling esoteric posters, crystals, amulets and the sort. Beneath a sign advertising the services of an "Internationally Renowned Faith-Healer" I see for the first time the name: "Renato Sergeant".

Is it just because this name sounds so improbable that it tickles my fancy?

Perhaps.

But I'm already dreaming up associations: the sergeant at arms, the sergeant with his Gunn, and my lovely Lady Agnew of Lochnaw (first name Gertrude), whom I've recently been admiring. She stares down at me again from her canvas with that equivocal gaze of hers.

Whether I claimed to be either tactful and discreet or honest and direct, in the end (which is to say the end of this book) I'd have to admit I was being neither. If I wanted to be faithful to my analyst, or rather to betray him – when these are one and the same – I'd have to do more than just report on him. I'd have to reconcoct him too. Not just any old how. No, I'd have to reconcoct him in a joke, one which I hope my reader may have shared.

Renato Sergeant. Pull the other one.

I nod to Renato on the poster, thanking him one final time. I turn from the shop towards the sunlight. Then I let out a bleat which echoes so loud up the porticoes that I can imagine it passing Eve in Paris, before it reaches across the sea towards the glens.